MILK

Edible

Series Editor: Andrew F. Smith

EDIBLE is a revolutionary new series of books dedicated to food and drink that explores the rich history of cuisine. Each book reveals the global history and culture of one type of food or beverage.

Already published

Forthcoming

Milk

A Global History

Hannah Velten

REAKTION BOOKS

Published by Reaktion Books Ltd
33 Great Sutton Street
London EC1V 0DX, UK
www.reaktionbooks.co.uk

First published 2010

Printed and bound in China by Eurasia

British Library Cataloguing in Publication Data

Velten, Hannah.
Milk : a global history. – (Edible)
1. Milk. 2. Milk – History.
3. Dairy processing. 4. Cookery
I. Title II. Series
641.3′71–DC22

ISBN 978 1 86189 656 8

Contents

Introduction

Milk is an ancient and universal food, sustaining us from birth. That mother's milk is pure and good is taken as read, but this history of a food and drink focuses on what happens past weaning, when animal milks are introduced into the human diet.

It is only a small percentage of the world's population that actually drinks milk – most preferring processed dairy products, such as butter, cheese and yoghurt – and animal milk is probably the most controversial of foods. Its qualities and associated dangers have been hotly debated since civilization began, which has resulted in milk either being demonized as a 'white poison' or exalted as a 'white elixir'. This situation has arisen because milk became a victim of its own success. As its popularity grew and fewer people had access to their own animals, milk had to be transported and this left it wide open to man-made abuses.

So, many questions now surround milk: is animal milk wholesome or harmful to humans? Is it a luxury or an everyday source of nutrients? Is it a food, a beverage, a cure-all or a ritual offering? Is today's processed 'milk' even milk as recognized by our ancestors? Does one pour the milk before, or after, the tea to make the perfect cuppa? The answers to these questions are about as opaque as milk itself.

Traditional milk delivery: Flemish dog cart and milk maid, *c.* 1900.

A vanishing milk tradition? Milkman delivering milk to your doorstep in Britain, 2008.

Apart from being controversial, milk is one substance that most readers will have memories (pleasant or otherwise) of consuming as a child; there is a certain nostalgia associated with milk that is rarely associated with other commodity foods. For instance, Westerners may think of frothy, animal-warm, creamy milk from the farm; drinking third-of-a-pint bottles of school milk (either half-frozen or lukewarm) through a waxed paper straw; silver foil-topped milk bottles waiting on the doorstep, sometimes pecked open by the birds; the whistling milkman, his electric float and the blue (or silver) milk crates; ice-cold milk straight from the fridge; the cream line in a bottle of milk; or blue and white ceramic milk jugs.

These utopian images of milk have mainly been consigned to the history books and it is only a tiny minority of societies that still drink milk straight from their animals. Today's global milk supply is more than likely supermarket-bought, packaged in poly-bottles, cartons or plastic bags/pouches (mainly in Canada, India and Central America) and homogenized to eliminate the cream line. But this is at least a step forward from the bacteria-ridden, adulterated and toxic milk of unregulated times past – the history of milk is certainly not dull, and its future is sure to be equally as turbulent.

I

The First Milk

Often described as 'Nature's Perfect Food', milk is the foundation of life for all newborn mammals. It is an opaque liquid, which is synthesized and stored in, and ejected from, the mammary glands of female mammals, solely for the purpose of nourishing their newborns. It is the first food of mammals, providing all the necessary nutrients for survival and initial growth until weaning.

Medieval sources thought that menstrual blood, diverted from the uterus during pregnancy to nourish the foetus, turned itself into milk after the baby's delivery[1] – in effect they believed that milk was twice-processed blood. However, milk is synthesized from nutrients within the animal's diet, which are withdrawn from the blood as it passes through the mammary tissue.

The composition of milk

Milk is mainly composed of water (over 85 per cent); the balance includes milk fats and milk sugars (mainly lactose) for energy, proteins (mainly casein) to provide amino acids, and vitamins and minerals. The relative amounts of these insoluble

The cow of choice: Holstein-Friesian dairy cows produce milk with a lower fat content after grazing lush pastures.

nutrients vary between species and breed of mammal (see Appendix) and are influenced by the mammal's diet and health, its general emotional state and the stage of lactation.[2] Pliny the Elder noted in *The Natural History* (*c.* AD 77) that, 'Every kind of milk is more aqueous in the spring than in summer, and the same in all cases where the animal has grazed upon new pasture',[3] and Samuel Pepys tells of one Dr Cayus, who was very old and lived only on woman's milk – actually suckled from the woman's breast – who 'while he fed upon the milk of an angry fretful woman, was so himself; and then, being advised to take it of a good-natured, patient woman, he did become so, beyond the common temper of his age.'[4]

The taste of milk varies between species and generally milk will also take on the odour of strong substances it comes into contact with, and becomes tainted with flavours eaten by the animal, such as the salty Cheshire cheese (Britain's oldest named cheese) which is produced from the milk of cattle grazing on the salty pastures around the Northwich and Middlewich areas. Milk also transmits the properties of the herbage which the animal eats, which can either be medicinal or poisonous. White snakeroot's presence in the milk of domestic animals killed many thousands of Midwestern Americans (including Abraham Lincoln's mother) in the early nineteenth century – the illness was known as 'the trembles' in animals, and 'milk sickness' in humans.

At the beginning of lactation, immediately after the birth of the young, the first milk to be secreted is called colostrum (also known as 'beestings' or 'first milk'). This milk is yellow to orange in colour, thick and sticky and particularly high in energy, protein and antibodies, but low in fat. It delivers highly concentrated food to the newborn and provides immunity against many harmful agents. After a few days, mature milk begins to appear, which is generally thinner and whiter in colour than colostrum. This mature milk increases in volume until it reaches peak production (the timing depends on the species), then production will slow as the young are weaned onto their adult foods.

Why animal milk?

Humans are the only species to consume milk past weaning. Why should this be the case? Part of the reason is that milk was available to our ancient ancestors. The domestication of animals such as the sheep, goat, cow, water buffalo, reindeer, camel, horse and ass allowed our ancestors access to a limited supply of milk. This meagre supply (compared with today's standards) gave human civilizations a big survival advantage: it provided sustenance in times of food and water scarcity in Africa and the Middle East; provided additional nutrients to a limited cereal-based diet (especially calcium and lysine); was an alternative to strong sunlight as a source

Woman milking a cow, from an early 13th-century bestiary.

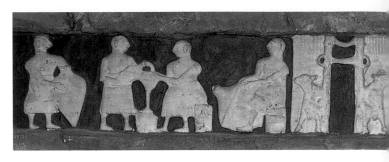

Early pictorial evidence of milking cows in the presence of their calves, c. 2500 BC, from the ancient city of Tell el-Ubaid, Iraq.

of vitamin D, which is necessary to strengthen bones (especially in North European populations); and was free from parasites, unlike water. Milking their animals was also a more energy-efficient way for our ancestors to convert vegetable protein (fodder) into animal protein rather than raising animals for meat.[5]

However, not all our domestic animals were found to be suitable for milking. Pig's milk, for example, was passed over, despite Pliny the Elder reporting that sow's milk was extremely useful in the treatment of tenesmus,[6] dysentery and consumption, and was very wholesome for females.[7] Pigs are scavenging omnivores and were regarded as 'unclean' by many civilizations. They are also difficult to milk as they have up to fourteen teats, many more than the usual two or four of other domestic animals, and they only 'let down' their milk for 10–30 seconds, compared with two to five minutes in cattle. Therefore it would have been impossible to milk pigs on an industrial scale. Though a nineteenth-century engraving shows a sow hoisted in mid-air by a harness contraption in preparation for milking, the idea never caught on.[8] In 2007 the animal rights campaigner Heather Mills wondered why drinking rat's, cat's and dog's milk hadn't become popular as a way to reduce the greenhouse gases

released by cattle[9] – the answer is probably for the very same reasons that pig's milk was avoided.

Milking the animals

It is a question that has dogged archaeologists for decades, but recent evidence has uncovered the most likely time and place that milking, a critical milestone in human civilization, was first practised. It was originally thought that sheep, goats and cattle were first domesticated (in that order) for their meat, hides and horn from about 9000 to 7000 BC in the Near East (the original site of domestication; modern-day Iraq), and then gradually exploited for their 'secondary products' of milk, wool and draft-power in the fifth millennium BC.[10] Evidence of milking was mainly inferred from the study of animal bones, which suggested that female stock were being kept beyond usual meat slaughtering ages, indicating that they were being kept alive longer for other purposes, such as milking.[11]

However, recent dating of milk residues found on pottery remains indicate that milking of animals may have occurred much earlier – during the seventh millennium BC and possibly earlier – and that the majority of milking occurred in north-western Anatolia (modern-day Turkey, far away from the Near East), where cattle dominated over sheep and goats as there was plentiful forage to support the larger species to produce their yields of milk.[12]

As for other species, the oldest known pictorial record of animals being kept in herds and milked is from the Libyan Sahara, where rock art shows domesticated sheep and cattle from about 5000 BC.[13] Bone remains of milking horses have been found in northern Kazakhstan in central Asia, dating from 3500–3100 BC,[14] and other pictorial evidence shows that milking was definitely in existence in Mesopotamia in the Near East, as seen in images on cylinder seals from Iraq (c. 2500–2000 BC), showing cattle being milked while their calves look on.

Early methods of milking

Irrespective of the species of animal being milked, early humans' first obstacle to gaining milk was to actually milk the animal successfully. Keeping the young away from the adult and attempting to hand-milk wouldn't have yielded any results because the adult wouldn't have 'let down' or released their milk. This release of milk from the mammary glands is totally reliant on the 'milk-ejection reflex'. This is an unconscious, physiological process which causes the hormone oxytocin to be released into the bloodstream to stimulate milk ejection after the sensory nerve endings in the nipple have been activated by butting and suckling.[15]

Early civilizations had to learn to exploit this reflex without the animal's young actually suckling – this was, and is still,

A pastoralist child initiating milk let-down by blowing air into the cow's vagina, 1982, East Africa.

done throughout the world with guile and trickery. If the young are alive, they may be allowed to suckle briefly first to start the milk flowing, and then the milker steps in to collect the milk. Sometimes even the presence of the young at the adult's head can be enough to elicit the response while the milker 'steals' the milk. If the animal's young has died, it will be skinned and the hide, scented with the young's urine, is draped over a pumpkin, stuffed with straw or draped over a person's back. Once the adult begins to lick the fake young, she will usually 'let down' her milk. If these stratagems fail, her hind legs are tied together (to stop her kicking) and then air is blown, using a special tube, into her vagina or rectum. In *The Histories* (440 BC), Herodotus describes this practised by the Scythians (the nomadic herders of Eurasia) on their mares: 'they insert a tube made of bone and shaped like a flute into the mare's anus, and blow; and while one blows, another milks. According to them, the object of this is to inflate the mare's veins with air and so cause the udder to be forced down.'[16] Other conditions that help to 'let down' milk are regular milking times, using the same milker each time and singing to the animals.

The act of milking

A relief of a sarcophagus at Ur dating from *c.* 2500 BC shows an early cow-milking scene where the men are seated behind the animal, reaching forward through the back legs to reach the udder. It seems that in the Near East and the cold parts of western Asia, milkers preferred to milk the cow from behind, while tomb scenes in Egypt after the early third millennium BC show cattle being milked from the side, which also seemed to be the usual practice in Europe and India.[17] Images of sheep-milking also show the milker either seated behind

Maltese milk-seller and his goat.

the animal or straddling it, facing the tail end, to hold it still between their thighs, while bending forward to reach the udder through the back legs – quite a feat of contortion. These methods of milking sheep and goats were used by all early civilizations and are still used today in Mediterranean countries.

There seems to be only one way of milking a mare: the milker kneels down on one knee, with a pail propped on the other thigh, steadied by a string tied to an arm. To reach the udder, one arm is wrapped behind the mare's rear leg and the other in front and a foal is used to start the milk flowing, but is pulled away by another person and kept close to the mare's side during the entire process. The milking of a camel is similar in that the calf is kept close, but because of the height of the camel's udder it is often necessary for the milker to stand on one leg with the raised leg bent at the knee and resting on the standing leg. On this bent leg rests the pot into which the milk flows – the milker using both hands in the milking process. Milking a reindeer required the effort of two people; one to hold the antlers (male and female reindeer both have antlers) and the other to do the milking.

A couple milking a mare out on the Mongolian steppe, 2006.

The balancing act required for milking a camel, Gobi Desert, Mongolia, 2008. Notice the calf's presence.

Lactose intolerance

Once humans had finally got hold of milk from their domestic companions, they came up against more problems. We are not talking about hygienic milk production here: if the milker needed lubrication to work the teats they would dip their hands in the milk already drawn and a surprising amount of dirt, insects and wool/hair would have to be strained from the pail or bowl after milking. It is probable that the milk would have contained plenty of bacteria.

Based on the properties of milk, aside from the risk of disease transmission, the experience for humans of drinking fresh milk straight from an animal would have caused rather uncomfortable and embarrassing reactions in our ancestors, such as diarrhoea, bloating, flatulence and stomach cramps. Western adults are now so used to drinking fresh milk that few realise what an unusual custom it is. Humans shut down production of the enzyme lactase, which digests the milk sugar lactose, after the age of six – this change may have evolved to stop adults and young children drinking milk designed for infants.[18] And being unable to digest milk lactose may well have put off early civilizations. Indeed, many human races in eastern Asia, Africa, southern Europe and the indigenous populations of the Americas and the Pacific have an aversion to milk; not just culturally, but biologically.[19] It has been estimated that 75–80 per cent of the world's population are unable to digest raw milk. It has also been suggested that the origins of the traditional loathing of dairy products in China dates back to the Ming dynasty's attempts in the fourteenth century to remove any trace of foods associated with the 'barbarian' Mongols who preceded them. So most Chinese did not come into contact with animal's milk after weaning from their mother's milk, and it is easy to see why the Chinese have described cheese unflatteringly as 'the mucous discharge of some old cow's guts, allowed to putrefy'.[20] Some civilizations found a way around the intolerance, such as the Indians, who took to boiling their milk, and many peoples found a preference for soured milk drinks, cheeses and/or butter, as the fermentation process and boiling of milk naturally breaks down the lactose.

However, most people within milk-drinking cultures produce sufficient lactase to digest lactose. This could be for several reasons, either genetic or environmental: milk drinkers who relied on milk for survival evolved genetically to become lactose-tolerant (via a mutation of a gene called LCT[21]) or continued exposure to milk from infancy through to adult life led to a continued tolerance.[22]

Spoilage of milk

Apart from reacting against fresh milk, another problem faced by early civilizations (and until recently) was the impossibility of keeping milk fresh for long outside the udder of the animal being milked. During the spoilage process, non-harmful bacteria (if you are lucky) feed on the milk lactose, which produces lactic acid, causing the milk to sour rapidly and curdle or ferment. This ordinary souring of milk produces harmless milk products, such as yoghurt; these are an acquired taste to Western palates, but especially beloved in the Middle East. However, milk that has been boiled and then left will putrefy (caused when the nitrogenous substances in milk break down) and become poisonous.

Spoilage was exacerbated in the high temperatures at the centres of domestication: milk was the 'ultimate local product, unable to be transported any distance'.[23] And due to the lactation cycles of the milking animals, milk was most plentiful in the spring and summer months when the animals gave birth to their offspring and pasture was abundant. With a glut of milk in the hot months, the situation was reversed in the autumn and winter when food was scarce. The animals would then 'dry up' and stop producing milk, leaving our ancestors without fresh milk for about four months of the year and having to rely on milk products, such as cheese and butter, which they made when milk was plentiful.

For these three reasons – lactose intolerance, seasonal fluctuations and perishability – fresh milk was a marginal drink and foodstuff for many civilizations.

Early use of milk

Fresh milk was essentially a food and beverage only taken by those who lived close to the land, such as shepherds and nomadic pastoralists, and the poor certainly would have subsisted on the barest necessities, of which milk was one. The Promised Land of Canaan was, after all, 'flowing with milk and honey', which symbolized its fertility and bountiful nature.

Much of the time fresh milk would be fermented or soured to produce alternative beverages, such as *kefir*, which is a fizzy, mildly alcoholic, yoghurt-type drink traditionally made by the shepherds in the Caucasus Mountains (on the border between Asia and Europe). It is made by storing sheep or goat's milk in a leather bag with *kefir* grains (a mixture of bacteria, yeasts and sugars), which is hung up and knocked with a stick every time someone passes it, causing the bag's contents to ferment.

Hillmen drinking *kumis* from a bowl, but it is prepared in a bag/pouch, north Pakistan, late 1920s/early '30s.

The wealthy, on the other hand, were quick to use milk in cookery. For example, cuneiform texts from ancient Babylonia, dated to around 1750 BC, show that milk or sour milk was used to prepare recipes such as goat-kid stew, 'tarru'-bird stew and bird pie. Milk often formed part of the stock in these festival dishes.[24] But this method of mixing meat and milk was not practised by all peoples, especially Jewish followers of the Mosaic code which stated that in kosher cooking, milk and meat should be kept separate, as dictated in the Bible: 'Thou shalt not seethe [boil] a kid in his mother's milk'[25] (also see the Maasai later).

It was also taught in the ancient system of traditional Indian medicine – Ayurveda or the 'science of life' – that meals cooked with milk and fish or meat should be avoided, although warm milk could be eaten with sweet tastes, such as rice, wheat, dates, mangoes and almonds. Neither, according to Ayurveda, should milk be drunk with anything sour, bitter, salty, astringent or with a strong flavour, as the milk would become indigestible – so it should never accompany a meal. However, in order to digest fresh milk properly, it must not be drunk cold. The milk should be boiled and allowed to foam up, then simmered over a lower heat for about 5–10 minutes. Heating the milk changed its molecular structure, making it much easier to digest, and while it was cooking, it was usual to add a pinch of ground turmeric, a pinch of ground black pepper, a cinnamon stick or a few pinches of ginger to reduce the heaviness of the milk and reduce any mucous-causing side effects.[26] This technique is still practised today.

With strict prescriptions on its preparation, the milk from the cow and water buffalo played a major role in the diet of Indian peoples – even today, India is the world's largest producer of milk, with an output of 102 million tons in 2007–8,[27] and buffalo milk accounts for more than 50 per cent of the nation's commercial milk supply.[28] The main breed of buffalo is known as the 'River' strain, which thrives on cheap and coarse tropical forages and produces copious amounts of bluish/greyish milk, which is denser and tastes creamier than cow's milk. One Indian society – the Todas of southern India – depends totally on its buffalo for milk, which they consume themselves and also sell for profit. They have roughly 1,800 buffalos supporting about 1,000 families in 60 different *mandus* or 'settlements'.[29]

Traditional dependency on milk

Apart from the Todas and most of rural India, there are plenty of developing countries and tribal cultures that have traditionally depended on milk as a staple of their diet. In Tibet, it is the yak, or the *dri* (female yak), that is milked by nomadic communities, producing a golden-coloured milk with a rich, deep flavour. But yields are low, with each *dri* only producing 200–300 kg per year (commercial dairy cows produce 20–30 kg a day). Although it is mostly children, the elderly and the infirm that drink the yak milk (boiled first), when the milk is abundant in the summer most milk is added to tea to produce 'milk tea', or it is soured and drunk or, alternatively, made into butter (often melted in tea), curds or cheese. Milk is also boiled with mushrooms to create a delicacy highly regarded by herdsmen.[30]

A feast is used to celebrate the first milking of the horses each year in Mongolia. It is the beginning of the season of 'White Food': a time of milk, cheese, curds and alcoholic beverages. Fresh mare's milk is generally not drunk as it is a strong laxative – Varro's *On Agriculture* from the first century BC

Milking the dri (female yak) in the presence of her calf, Mongolia, 2008.

notes this side-effect.[31] To make the pungent, mildly alcoholic drink known in Mongolia as *airag* and outside Mongolia as *kumis,* the fresh milk is put into bags made from leather or sheepskin and stirred with a big stick, which is as big as a man's head and hollowed out at the bottom.[32] The milk begins to sour and ferments after three days into *airag,* which is drunk at all celebrations. This drink was mentioned in the writing of the Flemish monk William van Ruysbroeck, who in 1253–55 visited the Mongol Court at Karakorum, then the most powerful city in the world and the hub of the continent. He describes the supplies of *cosmos* (as he called *airag*) coming into the Court and states that 3,000 mares supplied the milk.[33] The monk describes *cosmos* as:

> pungent on the tongue like râpé wine [poor quality wine] when drunk, and when a man has finished drinking, it leaves a taste of milk of almonds on the tongue, and it

makes the inner man most joyful and also intoxicates weak heads, and greatly provokes urine.[34]

Desert nomads, such as the Bedouin, were/are also reliant on their camels for milk – an essential source of fluid in drought conditions. Camel's milk is very watery when the camel is dehydrated and provides a nutritious and hydrating food for desert travellers.[35] Pliny the Elder stated that camel's milk was agreeable if diluted with three parts water (presumably this was milk from a hydrated camel).[36] Even if sheep and goat's milk was also available to the Bedouin, it was the camel's milk that was drunk – the other milks were turned into butter or cheese – because it was much preferred and considered to be healthier. Camel's milk is believed by the Bedouin to help cure hepatitis C, stomach pains, sexual disability and problems with digestion, and also increase immunities to disease.[37]

The Maasai of East Africa are one tribe of pastoralists who have traditionally lived off a diet of milk, meat and blood, all of which are derived from their cattle. In Maasai culture, there is a dietary prohibition against mixing milk and meat (because it is an insult to their cattle to feed off the living at the same time as feeding off the dead), so they will drink as much milk as they want for ten days – either drunk fresh or curdled – and then eat meat and bark soup for several days in between. But the milk can be mixed with blood, which is freshly tapped from the jugular vein of the cow with an arrow, and this bloody milkshake is used during ritual ceremonies and to give nourishment to the sick or weak.

The Sámi people of Finnish Lapland had an exclusive relationship with their reindeer, which provided them with relatively small yields of milk during the summer. The Sámi either drank the milk fresh, dried the whey by exposing it to heat (which was then eaten by softening it in coffee) or made the milk into cheese. Today the milking of reindeer is no longer routinely practised, but elderly Sámi remember a mixture of reindeer milk and herbs, such as mountain sorrel and/or the buds of the angelica flower, being heated into a porridge that could be saved in a keg throughout the winter.[38]

Greek and Roman attitudes to fresh milk

Not all civilizations took to drinking fresh milk, most notably the Greeks and Romans. Milk produced in the Mediterranean in ancient times, as well as modern times, was mainly that of the goat and sheep, which were species well suited to the hotter, more arid climate which did not support the lush pastures required by cattle. Their milks were often pooled together to increase volume and concentration, because goats yield several times more milk than sheep, but sheep's milk is more concentrated and naturally rich. These milks were primarily used for cheese-making.

Roman town-dwellers were not keen milk drinkers for several reasons. Most milk was produced on farmsteads outside the towns and cities, which meant it was difficult to keep milk fresh. Secondly, like the Ming dynasty mentioned previously, the intellectual Romans associated milk-drinking with barbarians (non-Romans) and wandering nomads who were uncultured and unrefined.[39] Herodotus tells of the nomadic Scythians who drank the soured milk of their mares (their slaves stirring the milk until it soured)[40] and Julius Caesar describes the first British tribes he encountered in 54 BC as '*lacte et carne vivant*' (living on milk and meat).[41]

However, it was inevitable that those Romans living in the countryside regularly drank milk from the sheep and goats they kept – practicality outweighed ideology[42] – and Pliny states that these country peoples flavoured their draughts of milk with a few sprigs of parsley.[43] But urban dwellers did enjoy one part of the milk: the 'beestings', which was listed by the Roman poet Martial in the *Epigrams* (AD 86–103) as one of the dishes which could be sent to party-givers as a gift, if one was short of money.[44]

If milk was to be taken as a drink then, according to Pliny, there were precautions to take, because it was 'known' that milk curdled in the stomach, which caused wind:

> The best milk of all is that which adheres to the finger nail, when placed there, and does not run from off it. Milk is most harmless when boiled, more particularly if sea pebbles have been boiled with it. Cow's milk is the most relaxing, and all kinds of milk are less apt to inflate when boiled.[45]

The *Roman Cookery* of Apicius shows several examples of how fresh milk was used in Roman, and Greek, cookery. These recipes range from the simplest directions for boiling salted meats in milk to make them sweet, to an extravagant entrée of fish, poultry and sausage in cream that used milk and eggs to set the mixture (which also included oysters, brains and sea nettles) into a terrine.[46] Milk was also employed in several dessert recipes, such as a Nut Custard Turnover, and it was also used in a more adventurous recipe called *cocleas lacte pastas* (snails fed on milk):

> Take the snails, clean with a sponge, and remove the membrane so that they can come out [of their shells]. Put into a vessel [with the snails] both milk and salt on one day and milk only on the remaining days, and clean out

the excrement every hour. When the snails are fattened to the extent that they cannot get back in their shells, fry them in olive oil.[47]

Soured or curdled milk (known as oxygala or melka) was eaten on its own, or mixed with honey or oil from unripe olives,[48] and it was made by simply adding sour milk, fermented fig juice or rennet to fresh milk.

Despite Caesar's rather derogatory observations of the Britons as milk drinkers, as with the Romans themselves, milk was mostly the drink of the poor in Northern Europe.

Northern Europe

Milk had played an important part in the diet of the people of Britain from the time when the first Neolithic farmers brought their domestic cows, sheep and goats into the country – although they would have suffered initially with lactose intolerance. The preference then was for cow's milk, but by the Bronze Age (due to the more open terrain, which had previously been covered in forest) more sheep and goats

English illustration of milking a goat and cattle, 12th century.

Stone carving of a milkmaid and cow being milked set into the wall of a house in Bruges, Belgium.

were kept and milked.[49] This inclusion of sheep and goat's milk in Britain's diet continued into the sixteenth century. According to the chronicler William Harrison in 1577, 'ewe's milk is fulsome, sweet, and such in taste as (except such as are used unto it) no man will gladly yield to live and feed withal' and goat's milk 'helpeth the stomach, removeth oppilations and stoppings of the liver, and looseth the belly.'[50] However, eventually the preference for cow's milk returned when the numbers of cattle increased due to the emergence of a fledgling dairy industry.

Throughout Scandinavia, Britain, France, Germany and the Netherlands, peasants and the poor relied on their animals' milk for sustenance (including the drinking of raw milk), while the wealthier, certainly by the sixteenth century, used milk and its products as useful additions to their cookery. They looked on milk generally with disdain, regarding the 'white meats' (milk, cheese and eggs), bread and pottage as the main food of the poor.[51] Sir Kenelm Digby, the English courtier and scientist, wrote in 1658 that 'there's not the meanest cottager but hath a cow to furnish his family with milk; 'tis the principal sustenance of the poorer sort of people.'[52]

But the kings of milk consumption were the Irish who, according to the sixteenth-century travel writer John Stevens, 'are the greatest lovers of milk I have ever met, which they eat and drink in about twenty different ways'.[53] The comic medieval Irish poem *The Vision of Mac Conglinne* shows that milk had been very much part of their diet for centuries as it speaks of 'very thick milk, of milk not too thick, of milk of long thickness, of milk of medium thickness, of yellow bubbling milk, the swallowing of which needs chewing . . .'.[54]

Milk reaches the Americas

It comes as no surprise then that European dairy consumers spread their milk drinking practices to the New World they discovered and colonized. The Spanish bought their cattle, and hence introduced milk, to Central and South American populations in the sixteenth century, but this milk was more commonly processed into cheese, as it was in the settlers' home country. Nowadays, milk drinking has become more prevalent in the Americas, especially in Argentina where 80 per cent of the population drink it thanks to waves of European colonization.[55]

However, the first written record of cattle arriving in Jamestown, Virginia in May 1611 (although there is some indication that it could have been in 1610[56]) showed the importance attached to milk by British colonists, and governor Lord Delaware wrote of his excitement that a further cargo of cattle was to arrive there the following year:

Milke, being a great nourishment and refreshing to our people, serving also (in occasion) as well for Physicke [medicine] as for Food, so that it is no way to be doubted, but when it shall please God that Sir Thomas Dale and Sir Thomas Gates shall arrive in Virginia with their extraordinary supply of one hundred Kine.[57]

And so, with the introduction of cattle to America, the US's turbulent relationship with milk began.

2

The 'White Elixir'

Moving on from regarding milk purely in terms of a functional food and drink, milk has also been traditionally seen as a mystical and precious substance; perhaps because of its scarcity. It was a pure, God-given product of the animals, which was revered for providing life to infants (whether gods, kings, saints or mortals) and for restoring the health of invalids. Milk was the 'white elixir' in many countries and mythologies long before its reputation became tarnished, and even today people who have trouble sleeping are advised to drink a soothing mug of warm milk before bed to ease them into sleep.

Purity of milk

It can be left to M. J. Rosenau, Professor of Hygiene and Preventative Medicine at Harvard Medical School in 1912, to explain the image of milk as a pure substance, associated with wholesomeness and well-being:

> Milk is everywhere and always has been held up as an emblem of purity. The fact that it is the sole food for babies during the first few months of life, its bland nature and

The whiteness of a drop of milk: a sign of its innocence and purity.

wholesome character, lend countenance to this belief.
Its very whiteness helps to give it a good character.[1]

In fact, anything described as 'milk white' was supposed
to be pure, as in John Dryden's poem *The Hind and the Panther*
(1687), where the milk-white hind stands as a metaphor for the
'infallible' Roman Catholic Church, whereas the panther, covered in spots, symbolizes the errors in the Church of England.
Another, more ancient metaphor for the purity of milk is seen
in the Hindu epic of the *Mahabharata*, where the gods and the
demons churn the Ocean of Milk in an attempt to obtain the
elixir of immortal life. This white Ocean of Milk is a symbol
of the mind or the human consciousness, which is seen as
being naturally pure, but its churning symbolizes the human

The association of milk with youth and purity, shown in the *Dairymaid*, Aleksei Venetsianov, 1820s, oil on canvas.

activity in the world which shapes the human mind; either producing poisons (human greed and selfishness) or the elixir (spiritual happiness). Among the treasures churned from the Ocean of Milk is Kamadhenu, the divine cow and mother of all cows. She was also a cow of plenty who could give her owner whatever they desired; she was otherwise known as the wish-fulfilling cow.

Hinduism

Milk is the primary reason for Hindu India's reverence of the cow, because she provides humans with the milk of life. And because of its association with the cow, milk is considered the highest form of gift to the gods. In the primary religious ritual of devotees of Shiva, the linga is honoured with offerings of flowers, milk, pure water, fruit, leaves and rice.

Milk has been consistently offered as a libation to other Hindu gods and on 21 September 1995 the global phenomenon of the 'Milk Miracle' occurred. It started in a temple in New Delhi when a Hindu worshipper made a milk offering to a statue of Lord Ganesh (the elephant-headed son of Shiva). When the man bought the spoonful of milk up to the trunk of the statue, it seemed to disappear as though the statue was drinking the milk. News of the miracle spread rapidly throughout the world and the same phenomenon was reported in temples in Britain, Canada, Dubai and Nepal. Small statues of Ganesh, Shiva and other deities were said to literally 'drink' buckets of milk within minutes and the 'miracle' became the best-documented paranormal phenomenon of modern times. By the following day the deities had ceased to accept milk. Hindus across the world regarded the miracle as a sign that the problems of the world would be overcome through faith – the milk-drinking was a manifestation of Divine Blessing.[2]

Milk is also used in Hindu purification rituals and one rather extreme example is that of the Thaipusam festival of faith and endurance, which provides Hindus with a chance to show penance or gratitude to Lord Murugan, the patron deity of Tamil-speaking regions in Asia. The ritual, which is banned in India, is carried out at the Batu Caves north of Kuala Lumpur in Malaysia and involves some self-mutilation (usually with hooks piercing the back or spears through the tongue) and offerings of milk in two-litre pots. The milk is carried on the pilgrims' heads up the 272 steps to the Temple Cave, where it is emptied out as an act of cleansing of the mind and soul, with the milk symbolizing purity.

In India, milk is especially associated with Krishna, the Supreme Person or Godhead, who as a child was raised by a group of cowherds. It is wholly appropriate that on Krishna

Samudra Manthan or the Churning of the Ocean of Milk, depicted at Bangkok airport, 2008.

Offering milk to Lord Shiva, Mayapur, West Bengal.

Kavadi-bearer (bearer of burdens) during the Thaipusam festival with his skin pierced with hooks attached to tiny milk pots, Malaysia.

Jayanti (Krishna's birthday) food and sweets prepared from milk predominate. Krishna is also connected with Nag Panchami (the Festival of the Snakes), when his victory over the Kaliya snake is commemorated. The festival occurs in July/August and is a day when snakes – especially the cobra, which is sacred to all Hindus – are offered milk to please them. Milk is either poured down snake holes found near to houses and temples, or bowls of milk are left out near holes so that the snakes may drink it. If a snake actually drinks the milk, it is considered to be extremely lucky for the devotee. By appeasing the snakes with milk (which they are believed to enjoy), the devotees and their families hope to avoid becoming victims of snake bites during the following season, when the rains wash the snakes out from their holes and make them very close neighbours.

Food of the Gods

Milk offered as a libation has not been confined to Hinduism. According to Pliny the Elder, Romulus, the mythical founder of Rome, poured libations of milk rather than wine, and used milk to douse funeral pyres. Perhaps this was because he and his brother Remus were suckled by a she-wolf, although it was more likely owing to a scarcity of wine.[3]

Milk was also sacred to the Egyptian goddess Isis (in her cow form) and a recipe for the sacred 'Milk of Isis' still survives, involving milk, almond syrup and strawberries.[4] This pink-tinted, sweetened milk represented the healing milk provided by Isis to nourish her son Horus, the deceased, and the pharaohs, who were regarded as her divine sons. Milk was carried in Isiac processions in a *situla* (breast-shaped vase), which allowed a stream of liquid to spill onto the earth as a

Silver didrachm
with wolf and
suckling twins
design.

consecrated and consecrating offering. Similar to the myth of
Isis providing milk for the pharaohs was that of the infant Zeus
(the supreme Greek god) and the infant Jupiter (the supreme
Roman god) being fed on goat's milk and honey – in some
versions of the myths the milk was provided by Amaltheia, the
divine goat. It thus followed that milk was often mixed with
honey and offered to the dead and to the gods of Greece and
Rome; the mixture was called *melikraton* in Greek.[5] In other
mythologies, such as the Norse, other animals were said to have
provided milk for the Gods: the goat Heidrun provided the
milk which formed the basis of the mead drunk in Valhalla
by the wounded Aesir (the principle race of Norse gods), and
the primeval cow Audhumla produced the four rivers of milk
on which the giant Ymir fed – the universe, according to Norse
mythology, was later created from Ymir's body parts.

Spiritual food

Milk was not just the food of the gods, but also of sages, seers
and saints. According to the Indian Ayurveda, the body is
dominated by one of three elements – *sattva* (equilibrium), *rajas*
(activity) and *tamas* (inertia) – which give specific character and
impulses to every person (much like the medieval European
concept of the four humours). These same elements are also
ascribed to different foods to explain their effect on the non-
physical aspects of physiology – the mind, heart, senses and
spirit. Of all milks, bar human milk, cow's milk is determined

Nicolas Poussin, *The Nurture of Jupiter*, mid-1630s, oil on canvas.

as the purest *sattvic* food, meaning that it is uplifting, yet stabilizing, acting as an aid to serenity and spirituality.[6] But it has to be drunk four hours after milking, otherwise it becomes *rajastic*: leading to stimulation and aggravation. Sages, saints and seers easily survived on *sattvic* foods alone (which was provided by local devotees), such as fresh milk or *kheer* (rice cooked in milk), as this diet led to the development of a higher consciousness. Milk would not induce worldly desires or distract their minds from their search for higher metaphysical truths.[7]

Outside of India, too, milk played a role in spiritual enlightenment. In Buddhism, rice pudding, made from cow's milk mixed with honey, was presented to Siddhartha Gautama (the 'Buddha to be') by a local village girl to break his fast. This milk dish gave him the strength to continue his meditation and he then reached enlightenment and became known as the Buddha, or the Awakened One.

In Ireland, one saint particularly associated with milk was St Brigid. She was washed in milk as a newborn baby and was nourished on the milk of a magical Otherworld cow, since she was unable to digest ordinary cow's milk. This cow was a white animal with red ears and it accompanied her around the farms on the eve of her Saint's Day (1 February). At this time of year there was little milk to be had from the cattle and the farm women would take a blessed candle to the cow's stall and singe the long hair on the upper part of the animal's udder in order to bring on St Brigid's blessing so that the cow's milk would be abundant in the spring. When May Day morning came, and the milk did indeed flow, the young people would visit farms and indulge in all types of rich milk dishes – syllabubs, curds, junkets and cream cakes.[8]

The magical cow that nourished St Brigid had many contemporaries. The Fuwch Frech was a magic Welsh cow, brindled black and brown, who would appear if anyone were in need of milk. She would fill the largest milk pail and then vanish, sometimes into a lake. Glas Ghaibhneach was the grey cow of Irish tradition. If either cow were struck, milked into a leaking bucket or otherwise offended they would disappear before providing all of their milk. One Otherworld cow, the Dun Cow, turned destructive after she was tricked out of her milk and she finally had to be slain by Guy of Warwick.

Bewitched cows and sour milk

In Northern Europe, milk was a precious substance and very vulnerable to all sorts of magical dealings, which were used to explain why cows stopped giving milk, or produced blood in their milk, or why milk 'went off'.[9]

Witches were primary targets, particularly in the guise of hares. To protect against their evil doings in Ireland, rowan

St Brigid depicted on a stained-glass window created by Evie Hone in St John's church, Malone, south Belfast, Northern Ireland.

wood (or mountain ash) was twisted around the milk pails and also hung at the cowshed door on May Day and garlands of primroses were hung on the cattle or strewn before the dairy door and trodden on before crossing the threshold. In Scotland, red ribbon was tied to the tails of cattle.

Other spirits, such as Tomte in Sweden and the hobgoblin Robin Goodfellow in England, were thought to cause all sorts of trouble in the dairy if they were not offered something milky to eat. As Samuel Harsenet, a commentator on religions, wrote in 1603:

> And if that the bowl of curds and cream were not duly set out for Robin Goodfellow, the friar, and Sisse the dairymaid, why then, either the pottage was burned the next day in the pot, or the cheeses would not curdle, or the butter would not come, or the ale in the fat [vat] never would have good head.[10]

The Brownie spirit also expected a bowl of cream or best milk and a cake smeared with honey each night otherwise he would cause havoc around the farm. The inhabitants of Shetland and the other Isles in Scotland poured libations of milk or beer through a holed-stone, in honour of the Brownie.[11]

Apart from trying to ward off fairies and witches, milkmaids also sang to their cattle in an effort to retain milk yields. The following nursery rhyme was originally a charm chanted to cows that were reluctant to give their milk, or were bewitched:

> Cushy cow [hornless cow], bonny, let down thy milk,
> And I will give thee a gown of silk;
> A gown of silk and a silver tee [cow-tie],
> If thou wilt let down thy milk to me.[12]

Medicinal food

On a more practical, rather than spiritual, level, milk has been seen as a medical remedy for invalids since ancient times. Pliny writes of fifty-four medicinal uses of milk, ranging from it being used as an anti-venom and to smother external itchings, to being used as an eye ointment. He states that asses' milk is the most efficacious (medically speaking), followed by cow's milk and then goat's milk.[13] Asses' milk did indeed secure its place in history as the ultimate milk for preserving health and curing complaints. It was a cure for gout and the ancients, according to Pliny, gave either asses' or goat's milk to their children before their meals – it was one of their great health secrets.[14]

In many Celtic remedies it was cow's milk, from a cow of one hair colour, that could be used as a remedy for consumption: one 'recipe' taken from *Arcana Fairfaxiana* (a manuscript

A poisoned glass of milk? Alfred Hitchcock's *Suspicion* (1941) puts milk in the spotlight.

of apothecaries' lore and housewifery, written in the sixteenth century) states:

> Take garden snails num. 5 break off the shells of them
> then boil them in a quart of new milk of a red cow till it
> comes to a pint and a half. Drink of this first and last and
> at all times of the day.[15]

Jumping forward to Stuart times in England, the noble
Lady Anne Clifford recorded that her ancestor, the twelfth
Lord Clifford, recovered from grievous illness after his wife
died by suckling milk from a woman's breast for about four
weeks and continuing the cure with asses' milk for several
months.[16] The greatly lampooned Lord John Hervey, who was
described by the satirist Alexander Pope as 'that mere white
curd of asses milk',[17] was also a devotee and ate a small quantity of asses' milk and a flour biscuit each day to prevent bouts
of epilepsy.

Since 1780, during the London 'Season', female donkeys
(jennys) would be out in the streets being milked directly for
customers. The oldest company in London was Dawkins of
Bolsover Street in the West End, who also hired out milch
asses to families, sending them across the country (from
Brighton to Scotland), accompanied with instructions on how
to treat them and how to milk them. As an ass would yield
about two pints a day, the London supply (from about 50
asses) could be got into a single churn.[18] In its heyday, asses'
milk was heralded by physicians as perfect for delicate and
consumptive patients, such as Elizabeth Barrett Browning,
who lived exclusively on broth and asses' milk a month before
she died of tuberculosis in Florence, in 1861.[19]

Asses' milk was also fed to babies. This was done on a
large scale at L'Hôpital des Enfants Assistés in 1880s Paris.

Certain City Macaronies, drinking Asses Milk, at Kentish Town.

at the Celebrated House at Kentish Town.

Drinking asses' milk in Kentish Town, London, *c.* 1760.

Doctor Parrot, who ran the nursery, described how the babies were fed using donkeys:

> The stables where the donkeys are kept are clean, healthy and well-aired; they open onto the nursing infants' dormitory. Treated gently, the donkey easily lets itself be suckled by the baby presented to it. Its teat is well adapted to the baby's mouth for latching on and sucking. The nurse sits on a stool to the right of the animal near its hindquarters. She supports the child's head with her left, with his body resting on her lap. With her right hand she presses the udder from time to time to help the milk to flow, especially if the baby is weak. The babies are nursed five times during the day and twice during the night. One donkey can feed three infants for five months.[20]

This process would have certainly avoided the problem of storing the milk and the intestinal upsets that killed so many children.

The cult of the 'Milk Cure' (or 'Goat's milk', 'Koumiss Cure' or 'Whey Cure') continued to rise in the mid- to late 1800s, especially in Russia and Germany, where practitioners of the cure (for invalids and infants) were forever advertising their residential stays in European newspapers. But *The Times* newspaper, in a book review, was less enthusiastic about the efficacy of the 'cures':

> The invalid has but to set foot in Germany to find himself surrounded by dozens of them . . . The most innocent and amiable of the many pleasant impostors of this world are our friends – the water cure, the milk cure, the grape cure, the cherry cure and the hunger cure.[21]

Then came the 'Sour Milk Cure' for old age in 1909, promoted by Nobel Prize-winning Professor Metchnikoff, which used the bacteria (*bacilli acidi lactici*) found in Bulgarian sour milk as an aid to eradicating the 'noxious germs in the intestines, and by overwhelming them set up that condition of body which is synonymous with perfect health and vitality'[22] – something like today's probiotic products. Products soon proliferated to provide the bacteria in more palatable forms, such as Lactic St Ivel Cheese and chocolate bonbons called Massolettes.

Today there are still promoters of the 'Milk Diet', which relies on drinking (preferably) raw milk for at least three weeks, with or without strict bed rest. It is said to cure chronic disease and is suitable for invalids, but not fit adults, who are struggling to get back to health – although there is a proviso in one classic text[23] that the diet is not suitable for acute disease sufferers, especially those with a fever; and there does seem to be a long list of possible side effects associated with living purely on milk, including constipation, nausea and unpleasant breath. However, it may be that a diet of milk does indeed lead to a long and healthy life; evidenced by Maria Esther de Capovilla from Ecuador, who in 2006 was the world's oldest woman at 116 years old – she firmly put down her great age to the nutritional wonders of donkey's milk.

Other qualities

Famously used by Cleopatra (69–30 BC), asses' milk was part of her beauty routine and Poppaea (30–65 AD), wife of the emperor Nero, continued the tradition. Pliny reported that Poppaea took 500 female asses (with foals) everywhere with her so that she could have a ready supply of their milk for her bath. Asses' milk was supposed to make her skin more supple and delicate, remove wrinkles and preserve its whiteness, and Pliny writes that some women washed their faces with it 700 times a day.[24] Milk was often added to a poultice of bread, which Greek and Roman women put on their faces at night 'to repair the effects of time as a cause of cutaneous aging',[25] and during Elizabethan times, lotions and ointments were prepared from, amongst other substances, asses' milk and were used to remove wrinkles and smooth skin.[26]

However, milk also had another magical property that was not only limited to improving the human condition.

Poppaea's milk bath as portrayed in Cecil B. DeMille's 1932 film *Sign of the Cross*.

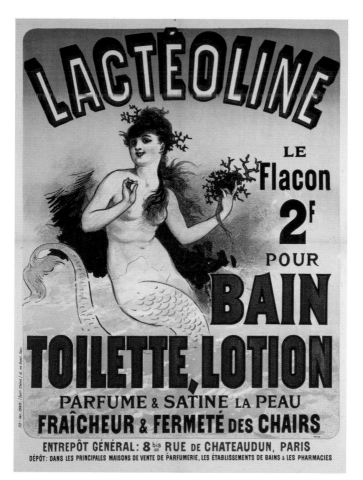

An 1880s advertisement for a toiletry using the beautifying properties of milk: 'Lactéoline pour Bain, Toilette, Lotion'.

Abd-el-Kader, the Emir of Mascara from 1832, wrote about the inhabitants of the Sahara who fed their horses with camel's milk, which

> has the special property of imparting speed to that degree, that, according to what is testified upon responsible and credible testimony, a man, by drinking it exclusively for a sufficient time, acquires such swiftness of foot, that he can successfully contend in the race with the horse.[27]

With all this glory surrounding milk it is surprising to learn that its reputation for 'purity' and goodness was tarnished – almost beyond repair.

3
White Poison

Milk sourced from the farm in rural communities was a staple of a rather bland, but wholesome diet. What happened in the Western world (and its colonies) in the mid-seventeenth century onwards was a rise in demand for milk from wealthier, urban areas. Whether this increase in milk use was due to a burgeoning population or whether new markets for milk were stimulated by the increase in milk production (from better quality cows on more nutritious feed) is debatable. What is clear, though, is that the demand for milk, although rising, was nothing like the demand today. Milk in the towns was still a casual purchase, bought in small quantities, and was not part of the average diet, mainly due to its price, since it was either produced in urban dairies or transported from nearby rural dairies. It was also still a seasonal product, with milk supply at its lowest in the winter.

Increasing consumption in Britain

In England, milk almost completely replaced almond milk in puddings and desserts on the tables of the more wealthy in the seventeenth century, and milk puddings became almost a daily staple.[1] Milk was mixed with either bread, sago, rice, oatmeal, sugar and/or spices, then baked; or it was added to flour and spices to make a milk pottage (a farmer's rice pudding); or sweetened milk was added to rennet to produce junkets (a loose pudding); or a syllabub was made from warm milk frothed over fruit, wine or spices. Also popular were spiced drinks of hot, sweetened milk curdled with wine or ale, called possets.

Fresh milk was drunk by infants, the elderly and invalids, but not healthy adults, although whey was considered to be very wholesome as a morning draught and London had several whey-houses, such as the New Exchange, which was patronized by Samuel Pepys in the 1660s (although whey, and eating curds, made his 'belly ake mightily'[2]).

By the end of the century, milk was being added to the new, costly hot beverages: tea, coffee and chocolate. Although milk had previously been omitted from tea, with the advent of fine china milk was added first to prevent the china from

Jean-Étienne Liotard, *Tea Set*, 1783, oil on canvas.

cracking. Adding milk or cream and sugar also lessened the bitterness of coffee and chocolate.[3]

Meanwhile, during the eighteenth century, the diet of the poor deteriorated due to land enclosure, bad harvests and price inflation. William Cobbett on his tour of the British countryside in the 1820s speaks of boiled, skimmed milk and bread being the diet of young children and its use in making puddings and bread and he also admits that, 'I have drinked little else for the last five years, at any time of the day. Skim milk I mean.'[4]

As the population of England and Wales quadrupled between 1801 and 1911 and people moved from the country-side into the towns (so that 80 per cent of people became town dwellers, rather than vice versa), milk became a commercially traded commodity and one of the pillars of the agricultural economy.[5] Because the cost of whole milk did not fall (as the prices of many other foods did in the nineteenth century), many sections of society were unable to afford milk, particularly the extra-rich milk from Channel Islands cows or special invalid's or nursery milk.

It was possible, at a cost, to get fresh, clean milk within London, but this was not the norm. Some cows were led around the streets and milked at the door, or it could be got from the eight cows which stood in St James's Park in the summer (and from four cows in the winter). The milk-sellers were licensed by the Home Secretary and the queues for the new milk consisted of children and their nurses and 'mostly young women . . . that's delicate'.[6] The 'Milk Fair' was abolished in 1885.

In general, cow's milk was far from being a 'pure' liquid in the nineteenth-century city. Indeed, it was downright dangerous and became an important cause of morbidity and mortality, especially for infants in the second half of the century.[7]

Milk for sale at 8 a.m. in St James's Park, London, 1859. The dairyman milks his tethered cows to provide sustenance for the children and nursemaids on their morning walk.

What was the problem? To cope with increasing milk demands, urban cowsheds and dairies began to open up and a network of milk deliveries were established to provide the perishable liquid to a growing number of customers. Unfortunately, in terms of public health, this was a tragic development because milk was produced in overcrowded, dirty cowsheds from diseased cows, transported in unhygienic conditions and stored without refrigeration. It was inevitable, as one commentator concluded, that this type of milk production would cause trouble: 'To separate the mouth of the baby from the teat of the cow by several hundred miles is often a serious matter for the baby, – for in the mean time the milk has deteriorated and may have assumed dangerous properties.'[8]

Urban dairies: condition of the cows

Horrendous descriptions of the living conditions of urban cattle abound, both in America and Britain. For example, even within the aristocratic parishes of London, there were numerous dairies, such as the 14 cowsheds within St James, Westminster in 1847. The Hon. Frederick Byng described two of these sheds:

> [They] range one above the other, within a yard of the back of the houses . . . Forty cows are kept in them, two in each seven feet of space. There is no ventilation save by the unceiled tile roof, through which the ammoniacal [sic] vapours escape to the destruction of the health of the inmates. Besides the animals, there is, at one end, a large tank of grains, a store-place for turnips and hay, and between them a receptacle into which the liquid manure drains, and the solid is heaped.[9]

Apart from the cows' living conditions, which provided neither fresh air nor exercise, the cattle were fed on the cheapest feed available. In London and other European cities this feed (and drink) was brewers' grains straight from the breweries. The grains were wastage left after the 'wort' (or sugary liquid) had been drained off – they were plentiful and cheap during the brewing season of October to May, but they could be preserved in pits.[10]

In the vicinity of New York and Brooklyn in the 1820s, many cowsheds were built near grain distilleries so that distillery-slops could be sent smoking hot via wooden gutters directly into the cow's troughs. The cows were fed up to thirty-two gallons each day[11] and by the 1830s, 18,000 cows in New York City and Brooklyn were fed on brewery or distillers' waste almost exclusively, with up to 2,000 cows in one dairy unit.[12]

Although high milk yields were produced from the grains, the cow's digestive system is not designed to take fermented products that are highly acidic and require no rumination, and especially not when taken hot. These grains made up the majority, or the complete, diet of many urban-kept cattle for months and months and cattle became sick and diseased relatively quickly. There were reports of cattle so ill that their tails rotted off and their skin broke out in gangrenous ulcers.[13]

Not only was the milk produced by these cattle of poor quality, but as William Cobbett wrote in 1821, it took on the flavour of the cow's feed: 'I have distinctly tasted the *Whiskey* in milk of cows fed on distiller's wash.'[14]

The first person to blame brewery and distillery dairies for the high infant mortality rate was the American Robert Milham Hartley in his *An Historical, Scientific and Practical Essay On Milk*, published in 1842.[15] He railed against the feeding of unhealthy and unnatural foods to cattle, which caused them to become thin, feverish and diseased and therefore only able to produce 'impure, unhealthy, and innutritious' milk.[16] He termed this milk 'slop-milk'[17] and talked of the milk as a 'blue, watery, insipid secretion'[18] which then was further diluted, coloured and drugged or medicated ready to be sold. He concluded that illness, particularly diarrhoea in children, resulted from drinking this poisonous milk.

Adulteration or 'toning' of milk

All parts of the dairy supply chain, particularly small shop-keepers and market sellers, boosted their profits (particularly in the later summer months when milk supply decreased) by

THE NEW FOUNTAIN OF DEMOCRACY.
Swill Milk for Hungry Suckers.

'Swill Milk for Hungry Suckers' – Swill milk and a diseased cow used for political leverage, image by John Cameron, New York, *c.* 1872, lithograph.

extracting the cream from the milk, after leaving it to stand for 12 hours, and adding water to the skimmed milk to make up the volume (milk was 'bobbed' or 'washed' in trade jargon[19]).

Most of this water came from 'the cow with the iron tail' (water pumps), therefore increasing the likelihood of contamination by dirty water. It was commonly thought that the liquid sold as milk was about a quarter added water,[20] although an analysis by Dr Arthur Hill Hassall in London between 1851 and 1854 showed out of 26 random milk samples from urban dairies, 11 were diluted from 10 per cent to 50 per cent. Dr Hassall concluded that 'There are but few articles of food more liable to adulteration.'[21]

As indicated by Hartley's *Essay On Milk*, it wasn't only water that was added to milk to 'stretch' milk supplies. The retailers also put additives in the milk to improve its colour, taste and/or smell. After the watering down of fresh milk,

THE CITY MILK BUSINESS.

MARY, THE KITCHEN-MAID. "Why, John, what's the matter?"
MILKMAN. "Ah, Mary! if we don't have rain soon, I don't know what we'll do for Milk!"

Cartoon showing the widespread practice of adulterating milk in *Frank Leslie's Illustrated Newspaper* (July 1859).

the milk would appear thin and have a bluish colour, so flour or starch was added to thicken it and chalk added to make it appear whiter, or annatto to give it a 'creamier' look. The juice from boiled carrots was often used to give a fuller and sweeter flavour to the milk and, most disturbingly, animals' brains were added to froth the milk up.[22]

The antiquarian John Timbs describes the additions to milk in his *Curiosities of London* (1855):

The adulteration of milk is a pestilential practice. The substances usually employed are water, flour, starch, chalk, and the brains of sheep, oxen, or cows; the brains have been detected with a microscope, shewing the nerve-tubes, their natural size being only about 1500dth of an inch in diameter; they are rubbed with warm water into an emulsion, and then added to the milk, or in larger proportion to London cream. This is a vile fraud imported from Paris. In Smollett's time[23] [early 1770s], London milk was described as chalk and water, with beaten snails for froth; the milkmen of our day have added treacle, salt, whiting, sugar-of-lead, annatto, size, &c.: the sugar-of-lead is most pernicious, being formed into carbonate of lead, which is held in suspension, a little giving a great bulk of water a milky appearance. A never-failing pump, or 'cow with the iron tail,' is indispensable to a Dairy establishment, to balance the statistics of demand and supply.[24]

Successive attempts to effectively legislate against the adulteration of milk failed to stop the practice, and it wasn't until the 1901 Sale of Milk Regulations in Britain, which stipulated that milk should contain at least 3 per cent fat and 8.5 per cent of other solids, that adulteration was curtailed.[25] However, the quality, or cleanliness, of the milk was never questioned at this time – it was more about preventing the customer being cheated, rather than their health being injured by disease-ridden milk.

Dirty and toxic milk

As already stated, the conditions in which urban milk was produced were filthy and full of foul air. Not only was the 'fresh' milk from the poor cows tainted in the first place (from the odours of the dairy and the flavour of the cow's food), but it was further contaminated by the dirt in the dairy and on dairy utensils, such as the pails and churns. Thoughts on hygienic production of milk did not really feature in reformers' calls for the cleaning up of urban dairies – more argument was directed towards cleaning up the cities of their noxious industries through a system of licensing.

Sanitary requirements by local authorities, starting from 1853 in London, did eventually make some headway in improving cowshed conditions although it took until the mid-1880s for licensing of well-regulated and clean cowsheds to become the norm. And it wasn't until 1873, over 30 years after Harley's wish to end the production of 'slop milk', that New York banned the distillery dairies.

However, the cost to urban producers of converting their cowsheds meant that many closed down and there was a greater reliance on rural milk, which was produced under no such regulations, which ironically made urban milk less likely to be contaminated than its rural cousin. One Medical Officer of Health who visited a cowshed three miles outside of London in 1906 was disgusted at what greeted him:

> He was taken to the cowshed, which to his horror he found to be at least three to four inches deep with filth, while the walls were splashed all over with cow dung and the flanks and teats of the cows themselves were in an abominable state. Under these circumstances he contented himself with viewing the animals from the door of the byre.[26]

What this meant was that the proportion of sour, dirty and infected milk on the urban market actually increased.[27]

Rural milk began to be shipped on railway trains into Manchester in 1844 and into London stations with special 'milk' platforms in 1846, such as the Somers Town milk dock

Railway milk trains running on the North Staffordshire lines at Uttoxeter, England, 1925.

alongside St Pancras Station. The import of milk in 17-gallon churns grew rapidly in the 1860s and '70s. But milk delivered in this fashion could easily be travelling from cow to station without refrigeration or proper storage (which allowed dirt and dust to enter the milk), for up to 24 hours – which in hot weather was more than enough time for pathogens to build up. Before reaching the customer, the milk would have been handled by a city dairy. They would have tested and smelt the milk and poured it into a large vat of pooled milk (from hundreds or thousands of different herds), strained it to remove dirt and slime, cooled it and then decanted it into unsterilized pails to be delivered.

It was hardly surprising that in 1899, a bacteriological examination of 50 samples of milk in St Pancras Station showed that only 32 per cent could be described as 'normal'. Of the rest, 6 per cent were 'dirty', 16 per cent contained an excess of microbes, 12 per cent were contaminated with excess leucocytes (white blood cells, which indicate the cow is fighting infection), 24 per cent had traces of pus and 10 per cent contained the tubercle bacilli (bovine tuberculosis).[28]

In an effort to prevent milk from spoiling, chemicals to preserve the milk were an innovation of the 1870s. These substances were particularly dangerous because although they stalled the souring process in milk, they didn't kill harmful bacteria. The preservatives used were also toxic to humans, such as the boric acid that was used in 'Kimberley's Food Preservative', the most readily used preservative in the largest dairies. Therefore customers presuming to buy 'fresh' milk were actually buying days-old, toxic and bacteria-laden milk. By the 1890s, formalin was also being used (its presence masked with sodium or potassium nitrate) and questions started to be asked about the issue of cheating customers out of 'fresh' milk, rather than questioning the toxicity of the milk.[29] In 1906, Upton Sinclair's exposé of the Chicago meat-packing district contained references to 'the pale blue milk that they bought round the corner', which was 'watered, and doctored with formaldehyde'.[30]

Milk was definitely the 'white poison' on many levels: it was produced from poor cows, in dirty dairies, diluted, adulterated, made toxic with preservatives and transported and stored without regard for cleanliness or coolness. And on its final journey to customers, Tobias Smollett, writing in 1771, gives probably the best (or worst) description of its treatment. The milk was

> carried through the streets in open pails, exposed to the foul rinsings discharged from doors and windows, spittle, snot and tobacco-quids from foot-passengers, overflowings from mud carts, spatterings from coach wheels, dirt and trash chucked into it by roguish boys for the joke's

An unusually hygienic-looking milkmaid from Sim's Dairy in London, 1864.

sake, the spewings of infants who have slabbered in the tin-measure which is thrown back in that condition among the milk for the benefit of the next customer; and, finally, the vermin that drops from the rags of the nasty drab that vends this precious mixture, under the respectable title of milk-maid.[31]

Delivering of the milk to customers was women's work and little had changed by 1868 when Arthur Munby (who was a rather perverse chronicler of working women) described the workings of a milkmaid in Hyde Park Square, London. She carried her milk (about 48 quarts in all) in pails hanging from a harness, on a wooden yoke made to fit her shoulders, which displayed the name of her 'master', the dairyman. She also carried many individual metal cans, of different sizes, with her to leave with customers on her rounds. At six o'clock in the morning, before any maidservant or house gates were unlocked:

[She] left her pails by the lamp post, took with her one of the smaller cans, and with her yoke still on her shoulders and the harness hooked together across her chest she tramped down the street, her iron-shod boots ringing loudly . . . she carries with her a coil of stout string with a hook at the end. Taking this out of her pocket she hooked it on to one of the little cans and rapidly unwound it through the railings, let down the can into the area, jerked the hook off, and drew up the string, leaving the can behind.[32]

The cans were collected again at the end of the day and returned to the dairy, before the milkmaid could finish for the day. Then the milk would further deteriorate in the customer's home without proper refrigeration or storage.

Infant mortality due to milk

It was hardly surprising that drinking milk was an iffy business and the stigma of unfit milk persisted, even if many illnesses were not actually caused by milk. The greatest killer in infancy throughout the nineteenth century was infantile diarrhoea, which had a peak incidence in the summer (hence it was also termed 'summer diarrhoea'), and it was felt that contaminated milk was partly responsible for the rising mortality rates of London infants, especially in the 1890s,[33] and infants in the United States.

This was a major social concern at the time. In 1874 the *New York Times* stated, 'It will be generally conceded that the health of all great cities is dependent, in no small measure, upon the quality and purity of the milk generally consumed. In the case of infants, the dangers from impure milk cannot be exaggerated.'[34] And statistics from the United States Census of 1900 seemed to confirm this statement: in New York City the death rate for infants under one year was 189.4 per 1,000 live deaths, and because the majority of deaths were due to intestinal disorders and diarrhoea, feeding of infants with cow's milk was one cause singled out.[35]

But why were infants, in particular, coming into contact with contaminated cow's milk? Between 1840 and 1920 there was a move in Western countries away from breastfeeding towards bottle-feeding with relatively cheap cow's milk, artificial infant formulas and condensed milk.

The decline in breastfeeding from the 1840s, according to the author of *Nature's Perfect Food: How Milk Became America's Drink* (2002), was due to working-class women either producing too little milk due to food scarcity or being away from the home working; middle-class and upper-class women artificially feeding their babies because of societal mores; and the fact

'It looks like a tough fight for the little fellow', Gaar Williams's cartoon from the *Indianapolis News, c.* 1910.

that women who moved into urban areas were removed from the traditional female communities where breastfeeding was part of the normal way of living.[36]

Alternatives to breast milk

By the mid-nineteenth century, cow's milk was regularly being fed to infants. However, by then there was an appreciation of the chemical composition of milks and it became obvious that cow's milk was proportionally higher in fat and protein but lower in sugar than women's milk.[37] Therefore, to aid the baby's digestion mothers were advised to make up 'Sugar of Milk' for bottle-feeding:

Cow's milk may be assimilated to human milk by dilution with water and the addition of sugar of milk . . . When necessary to bring up a child by hand from birth, sugar of milk is more suitable to begin with. Formula: One ounce of sugar of milk should be dissolved in three-quarters of a pint of boiling water, and mixed as required with an equal quantity of fresh cow's milk. The infant should be fed with this from the feeding-bottle in the usual way. Care must be taken to keep the bottle, etc., perfectly clean.[38]

Therefore cow's milk, which was usually contaminated if relying on urban supplies, became increasingly used as a substitute for breast milk. There were other 'milk' options open to mothers, notably canned condensed milk and infant formulas, but these didn't improve the health of infants either.

Not every mother could afford fresh milk (not even the cheap diluted liquid) and many working-class families went for the cheaper 'condensed' tinned milk instead, which was introduced on a commercial scale in the 1870s. The idea for a portable, sterile, canned milk product came to Gail Borden (its inventor) during a transatlantic trip in 1851, when the cows in the hold became ill and he witnessed several children die after drinking the contaminated milk. In 1856 Borden eventually gained his patent (after three years of rejection) for condensed milk, which was fresh milk boiled at a low temperature in airtight vacuum pans, leading to about 65 per cent water evaporation. The concentrated milk product, when canned, would not spoil.[39]

Borden opened several small processing units, but sales were sluggish: consumers were used to milk which was usually watered down and full of artificial colour – the condensed milk was just not to their liking. However, the undaunted Borden found financial backing and formed a partnership called the New York Condensed Milk Company in 1858. Rather luckily for Borden, an advertisement for his condensed milk appeared in the same issue of *Leslie's Illustrated Weekly* that broke the news of 'swill milk' and 'slop milk' and milk adulteration, leading to a steady market for their sanitary (and cheaper) product. Then in 1861, during the Civil War, the US government ordered 500 lbs of condensed milk for the Union Army as part of their field rations – it was mainly used in coffee, which was drunk in huge quantities. As the conflict grew, the orders increased and Borden had to license other manufacturers to keep up with demand. After the war, to distinguish his product from its new competitors, Borden adopted the

Chubby, healthy babies were the advertising image of choice for Eagle Brand Condensed milk, 1883.

American bald eagle as his trademark and called his milk 'Eagle Brand'.[40]

Before long, condenseries were springing up everywhere, especially in Switzerland[41] and Wisconsin, where cows produced more milk than could be sold fresh. One version of condensed milk saw it sweetened with cane sugar (about 45 per cent of the total volume), which not only acted as a preservative against bacterial growth, but also made it more unctuous and palatable. And by the 1880s full-cream varieties of sweetened milk were being outsold by skimmed milk varieties, which used skimmed milk from butter factories. High-pressure advertising was being used to convince mothers of the benefits of bottle-feeding with the diluted condensed milk (usually twelve parts water to one part condensed milk[42]). By 1892 condensed milk of all types (sweetened and unsweetened – also known as evaporated milk) accounted for 11.6 per cent of London's milk intake.

However, by the late 1880s and early '90s it became clear that there were serious health implications for babies and infants whose diet was centred on condensed milk. Despite the milk being sterile, the skimmed milks were low in fat, proteins and vitamins A, C and D and lacked the calories required by infants. It was said that an infant who was reliant on these milks was likely to suffer from rickets and scurvy (although this was not true) and other diseases associated with malnutrition. Sweetened versions also contained excessive sugar contents, which frequently led to flatulent distention of the intestines, leading to hernia.

Public anxiety about its use, or misuse, was voiced in America and Britain. In 1894, the Select Committee on Food Products Adulteration in London discussed the evidence and shortly after, it was made compulsory for such milks to be labelled as 'Not suitable for feeding to infants or young children'.[43] However, the manufacturers continued to promote their product despite the warnings on the tin and in a newsletter called *Nutrition and Health*, published by The Borden Company in 1924, there appeared a recipe for diluting Eagle Brand condensed milk, with the resulting drink to be used as a substitute for fresh milk at school breaks.[44]

Not only did condensed milk lack the necessary nutrients for an infant, but illness (usually diarrhoea) frequently occurred when flies were attracted to tins of the sweet milk left open between feeds.

The other product to rival diluted cow's milk was infant formula – which was either milk-based and diluted with water, or was mixed with cow's milk. There was a huge surplus of skimmed milk in the nineteenth century (there was no market for low-fat milks then). This caused skimmed-milk manufacturers to find a product that would compete with condensed/canned milks, and which would save on packaging costs and preserve milk for longer. The answer was dried cow's milk powder.

Milk powder became synonymous with infant formulas. In 1867 two manufacturers fought to claim the invention of infant formula milk: Liebig's Soluble Food for babies was a formula that was mixed with diluted cow's milk, which 'perfectly' matched mother's milk; whereas Henri Nestlé invented a dried milk- and malt-based infant formula, Nestlé's Milk Food (originally called Farine Lactée Nestlé), to which water was added. Nestlé's product was marketed on a larger scale than Liebig's after he successfully raised a premature baby, who could not tolerate its mother's milk, on the milk gruel.

Numerous infant formulas then came to the market and they were mercilessly marketed in women's magazines, convincing not only mothers but doctors too. In the UK in 1908, a new dried milk for infants called 'Cow and Gate Dried

Advert for Nestlé's 'Complete food for children', made of cow's milk,
wheat flour and sugar, *c.* 1895.

Pure English Milk' was being promoted. 'Mother, is Your Baby Thriving?' and 'Babies Love It!' were familiar advertisements to all at the outbreak of the First World War.[45] Infant formulas were also shipped and marketed all over the world, particularly to less economically developed countries.

However, with their increasing use there was not a significant decrease in infant mortality. The poorer sections of society mainly used condensed milk and infant formula, and therefore they were more likely to use contaminated water (or milk) to dilute the products, and were also more likely to mix up weaker solutions than directed in order to save money. Nutritionally and hygienically, cow's milk in whichever form did not prove to be better than breast milk for raising infants and feelings against infant formula ran so high that in an address to the Rotary Club in Singapore in 1939, entitled *Milk and Murder*, Dr Cicely Williams outlined the dangers of bottle-feeding with inappropriate breast-milk substitutes, which she had seen in the country:

> If your lives were embittered as mine is, by seeing day after day this massacre of the innocents by unsuitable feeding, then I believe you would feel as I do that misguided propaganda on infant feeding should be punished as the most criminal form of sedition, and that those deaths should be regarded as murder.[46]

So, with milk labelled as 'White Poison', how on earth did society solve the issue and allow the liquid to become the number one drink in Western countries by the mid-twentieth century? Milk had to undergo a transformation, which saw hygienic production, heat treatments, nutritional science and marketing work its magic on the widely-despised milk.

4
Solving the Milk Question

By the 1860s, health professionals and reformers were looking at solutions to the increasing infant mortality and its
connection with dirty urban milk supplies. The problem with
milk was colloquially termed 'The Milk Question' and the
answer, or solution, was to purify the milk supply, but how to
do this caused some controversy.

'The Milk Question' defined and
how to solve it

The problem with milk was that it was difficult to buy due
to its scarcity (especially in the winter) or it was unaffordable
(especially in the poorer neighbourhoods). If families could
buy it, and it was normally wealthier families that could, there
was a good chance that it had already gone sour, was adulterated or was full of bacteria due to the long chain from cow to
consumer that made milk a haven for bacteria, especially
those responsible for tuberculosis.[1] Yet public health officials
promoted milk as a food staple for children, and increasingly
adults, because the emerging science of nutrition identified
milk as containing the widest range of vital nutrients at least

Gerard David, *Virgin and Child with the Milk Soup*, c. 1515, oil on panel.

cost to the consumer – in particular, its content of calcium and phosphorus to promote healthy bone growth. As US health professional M. J. Rosenau stated in 1912: 'The milk question is then a real problem of first magnitude worthy of our careful thought and attention.'[2]

Milk reformers in the US came up with two differing solutions. The solutions focused on the opposite ends of milk production: the former on clean milk production (prevention) and the latter on killing off any pathogens in raw milk (reactive). But Rosenau's ideal solution was a mixture of the two: 'To keep milk clean, we need inspection. To render milk safe, we need pasteurization . . . A milk supply, therefore, that is both supervised and pasteurized is the only satisfactory solution of the problem.'[3] However, in the absence of official action, 'certification' of clean dairies and 'pasteurization' coexisted in the US from the 1890s until the 1910s.

The knowledge of bacteria

The crux of the problem was the bacteria which was present in milk. It wasn't fully appreciated that milk could transmit infectious diseases and viruses to humans until 1857 when Dr Michael Taylor, Medical Officer of Health for Penrith, England, attributed an outbreak of typhoid to milk infected by a human sufferer. In 1867 he also traced an epidemic of scarlet fever (scarlatina) to a single cowkeeper whose child was infected.[4] Louis Pasteur's work in the early 1860s showed conclusively that particular microbes actually caused particular diseases and it became widely believed that milk could be transmitting diseases, most notably tuberculosis, typhoid fever, scarlet fever, diphtheria and septic sore throat.[5] Even with hindsight, there is no way of telling whether raw milk really was responsible for much of the infant mortality of the period, but public health authorities certainly perceived milk as being one of the main culprits. Milk seemed to be the perfect vector for disease. As Rosenau stated, 'bacteria love milk. They love it as much as the baby does. Milk is the perfect food for the growth and development of germs. They grow in milk at a prodigious rate, and hence the danger is sometimes very great.'[6]

Prevention through inspection

The New Jersey paediatrician Henry L. Coit began to look at how to secure clean milk for his patients after finding out that the milk he had been buying for his son was actually produced by a dairyman who was in contact with three people diagnosed with diphtheria. Coit was so concerned that he pioneered the 'certified' movement, which called for the inspection of dairy farms to ensure that they produced clean raw milk that was suitable for infants and the infirm to consume.

His inspection criteria began with the cows, which he stated should be in good health and he recommended they should also be free from bovine tuberculosis. Of all the communicable diseases spread in milk, tuberculosis was the greatest threat to human health. Bovine tuberculosis is an infectious disease of cattle and between 1907 and 1914 the UK's Royal Commission on Tuberculosis (amongst others set up in different countries) conclusively proved that the bovine strain of tuberculosis was transmissible to humans via cow's milk. Further American studies showed that between 5 and 7 per cent of all human tuberculosis could be attributed to the bovine type of bacillus. This bacilli entered the milk either directly from the udder, from coughed up bacilli, via faecal matter or during the pooling of milk supplies. In general, between 1906 and 1910, 8.3 per cent of urban milk supplies throughout the US contained the tubercle bacilli[7] – it was a disturbingly widespread occurrence.

The emerging science of bacteriology provided a test, known as the tubercle test, to detect the presence of tuberculosis in cattle. It involved injecting the cattle with a dose of tuberculin (which is harmless to a normal animal, but produces a reaction in a cow with tuberculosis) and taking a series of body temperature readings after about 10 hours. Reactors

A late 1930s WPA Art Program poster in Ohio encouraging truck drivers to report communicable diseases, which could contaminate a dairy's milk supply, to the Food and Drug Administration.

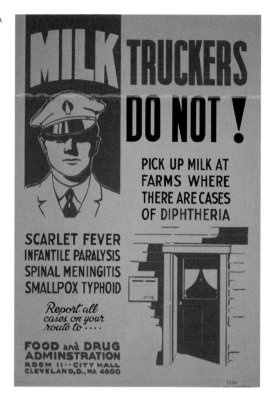

MILK TRUCKERS DO NOT !

PICK UP MILK AT FARMS WHERE THERE ARE CASES OF DIPHTHERIA

SCARLET FEVER
INFANTILE PARALYSIS
SPINAL MENINGITIS
SMALLPOX TYPHOID

Report all cases on your route to ....

FOOD and DRUG ADMINSTRATION
ROOM 11··CITY HALL
CLEVELAND,O., MA 4600

OHIO

showed an increase in temperature and/or swelling around the injection site and were removed from the milking herd, and suspicious cases were retested six weeks later with double the original dose of tuberculin. While this was a step forward for tuberculosis prevention, there was an argument that by supplying tubercle-free milk to children (especially) they could not become gradually immunized to tuberculosis through exposure to the bacillus in the milk supply.

Aside from the health of the cow, Coit also wanted the inspection to look at the milking practices, the housing conditions and the storage of milk, which were all checked for

Clean versus Dirty milk production – educational placard from
Philadelphia Milk Show, 1911.

cleanliness and standards of hygiene. The milk produced was to be also subject to periodical chemical analysis (to prevent adulteration) and bacterial counts.

Another weapon in the arsenal against bacteria was this bacterial count, which measured the number of bacteria per cubic centimetre in the milk. It gave clues as to the cleanliness of the milking process and the condition of the dairy, the temperature at which the milk was stored and the age of the milk. It was, at the time, the easiest and cheapest method for determining the general quality and grade of milk. However, because milk was studied in the laboratory it was a lengthy process and it was also difficult to determine the source of high bacterial counts from a sample of pooled milk.

Coit stipulated a standard of 10,000 bacteria per cubic centimetre for his 'certified' milk and while these numbers may seem frighteningly high, these counts also included 'good', naturally occurring bacteria. The milk had to be also bottled on the farm in the new glass milk bottles which had been invented by Dr Hervey D. Thatcher in New York in 1884. These bottles were topped by porcelain discs held on by wire and they protected the milk from contamination and adulteration.

Through vigorous campaigning, Coit was able to establish the Medical Milk Commission in New Jersey and this group delivered the first bottle of officially 'certified milk' in 1894. Many reformers started to push for certification in many cities, either through voluntary codes or through government regulation and legislation. By 1906, the movement's zenith, 36 Milk Commissions in the US were supervising and taking bacterial counts of milk from hundreds of dairy farms. However, this milk, due to the manpower required, was two to four times as expensive as ordinary milk and out of reach for most Americans. At its peak, only between 0.5 and 1 per cent

The Thatcher Milk Protector did what it said on the bottle – preventing adulteration and contamination.

of milk sold in major American cities was certified[8] and there was no guarantee that the milk was definitely safe.

Another grade of milk known as 'inspected' set its bacterial count at 50,000–100,000 bacteria per cubic centimetre (depending on the State) and milk was guaranteed (but not always) 'tuberculin-tested'. It was slightly cheaper than the 'certified' milk, but again, it could not claim to be completely pure.

However, the pro-pasteurization groups guaranteed the safety of their milk as the process of heating the milk killed off the tubercle bacilli, and other harmful bacteria, it could have been harbouring. Rather than preventing bacteria, pasteurization focused on purifying raw milk.

Pasteurization

When milk was identified as a vector of diseases, the chemist Franz Ritter von Soxhlet in 1886 furthered Louis Pasteur's work on the 'pasteurization', or heating, of wine and beer and developed a method of eliminating microbes from milk by heating it to a prescribed temperature. His methods were soon developed and the first systematic method of pasteurization was 'Vat' or 'Holder' pasteurization, which heated the milk in a large tank to 145°F (63°C) for 30 minutes. This process only allowed small-scale heat treatment. Then 'Flash' or 'High Temperature Short Time' (HTST) pasteurization became the industry standard (and is still used today). This required rapidly heating a continuous flow of milk to 161°F (72°C) for 15 seconds, followed by rapid cooling. This could be done on a commercial scale.

In 1892 the New York businessman turned philanthropist Nathan Straus set up his Pasteurized Milk Laboratory in New York, and in June 1893 opened a 'milk depot' to distribute the subsidized milk to the city's poor mothers in an effort to prevent 'summer diarrhoea' in their infants. The following year he opened another three throughout the city. He argued that pasteurization killed all pathogens, without changing the taste or nutritional quality of the milk, unlike sterilization[9] – the precursor of pasteurization. This process had involved the boiling or scalding of milk up to three separate times, but this changed its taste for the worse and killed off some of its vitamin content without making it more digestible. It was also a lengthy, involved process and it fell out of favour in America by the late 1890s.

So Straus became pasteurization's chief advocate and by 1916, his milk stations had dispensed about 43 million bottles of pasteurized milk, which cost him more than $100,000 a

Apparatus for pasteurizing milk in a state-of-the-art American dairy, *c.* 1910.

'The Consultation in Doctor Variot's Surgery', from Jean Geoffroy's triptych *The 'Drop of Milk' Clinic in Belleville*, 1901, oil on canvas.

year to subsidize.[10] He demanded compulsory pasteurization on all milks, including 'certified' milk. It was not only a matter of economics (as 'certified' milk was so expensive) but also of practicality, as pasteurization seemed to be a quick, technical fix that would make all milk safe to drink. Other groups, such as the Women's Municipal League and the Academy of Medicine, supported him in the need to pasteurize New York's milk supplies and other countries followed this lead in providing rations of heat-treated milk to the poor, such as at the *gouttes de lait* (literally, 'drops of milk') in France.

However, there were concerns about pasteurization. Many doctors and social reformers believed that pasteurization would destroy, or at least reduce, the nutritional properties of milk and also allow 'dirty' milk to be passed off as 'clean' milk, and so deflect attention away from producing pure milk in the first place. Others claimed that heating milk would 'devitalize' it, or kill off the 'life' within it.[11]

These two movements (certifying and pasteurization) co-existed relatively peacefully from the 1890s into the 1910s, each being advocated as the way forward for clean milk. But eventually, despite the strong voices of the raw milk advocates, compulsory pasteurization of all milks except 'certified milk' became law in most US states and municipalities by the 1940s. This was mainly due to the fear of bovine tuberculosis spreading to humans through milk and the advent of pasteurization on a commercial scale (using the HTST method). Chicago led

Milk bottles leaving the purifying heat of the sterilizer in a large dairy in New York State, c. 1910.

the way in 1908, closely followed by New York City on 1 January 1912, which was then importing two million quarts of milk from 44,000 farms in seven states.[12]

The UK's solution to the Milk Question

The situation in the UK was decidedly slower-paced and virtually all British milk in 1912 would have been outlawed as unfit for human consumption in New York City.[13] In fact, the UK was behind other European countries as well, including France, Germany and Denmark and for most people in the UK the consumption of raw milk remained a significant hazard until after the First World War and into the 1920s.[14]

This gridlock was not due to apathy on the part of reformers. Groups such as The National Clean Milk Society, founded by Wilfred Buckley in 1915, called for nutritionally healthy, disease-free milk, rather than just cheap milk:

> British mothers . . . have a right to clean milk for their children, and the government must see to it that arrangements are made, not only for the proper housing of the people, but also for the proper production and handling of the children's food – clean milk.[15]

But, apart from anti-pasteurization propaganda, one milk historian puts some of the blame for Britain's slow uptake of pasteurization firmly on the shoulders of the powerful group of UK dairy farmers who strongly opposed compulsory pasteurization mainly on the grounds of cost, but also because they resented intrusion into their business by 'ignorant and sometimes officious' city persons, 'whose knowledge of farming matters, and particularly cattle, is probably non-existent'.[16]

The farmers' political lobbying, and the First World War, stopped most proposed legislation regarding milk safety until the 1922 Milk (Special Designations) Orders and its 1923 Amendment. But this law did not require compulsory pasteurization; rather, it introduced a voluntary grading system for milk production focusing on whether the cows had been tested as tuberculin-free and the milk bottled and sealed on farm (the 'Certified' grade), the cows tested as tuberculin-free (the 'Grade A' grade), the cows tested as tuberculin-free and the milk delivered in sealed (tuberculin tested) churns (the 'Grade A (TT)' grade) or whether the milk had been pasteurized (the 'Pasteurized' grade). All of these types of milk were more expensive than raw milk and the system was fairly confusing.

Many of the larger dairies (like United Dairies) decided to pursue pasteurization as it instilled a public confidence in milk which saw demand for their milk grow. But thousands of small producers did not bother with pasteurization or grading, and because milk distributors mixed milk from dozens of farms, a small amount of infected milk could contaminate a whole batch. Milk-borne infectious diseases, especially bovine tuberculosis, were still a significant problem in the early 1930s when about 2,000 infants were still dying from tuberculosis transmission in the UK[17] and it was only through concerted efforts of reforming bodies such as the People's League of Health (PLH) that government policy finally looked at compulsory pasteurization. The PLH were especially concerned because of the subsidized milk schemes being launched in state elementary schools which would expose children to the dangers of tuberculosis and other milk-borne diseases.[18]

The compulsory pasteurization cause was also helped by medical professionals, who countered arguments about pasteurized milk losing its nutrients with research that showed vitamins remained unharmed by heating (except Vitamin C, but there was so little in raw milk that it was irrelevant). However, it wasn't until after the Second World War, when the health of the nation was top priority and farmers had a milk surplus, that the Milk (Special Designations) Act in May 1949 eventually made compulsory pasteurization the standard treatment for all milk. When compared with the us, where 50 per cent of milk had been pasteurized by 1912, and 95 per cent by the 1930s, the uk was certainly more lax about its food security.[19]

Now with a guaranteed supply of clean milk, it was time for the British government to make milk one of the cornerstones of its welfare policy. Milk, as shown by nutritional science, was the cheapest food available and the Government's aim was to increase consumption in infants, children and adults to produce a new, healthy generation of milk drinkers. Perhaps the most obvious path to getting milk into children was the extension of subsidized school milk, which logically followed on from 'welfare milk' (subsidized milk for infants from poor homes).

School milk

Milk had been subsidized in British elementary schools to some extent since the 1920s, when readily available milk (mainly heat-treated) was deemed to be a 'nutritionally rich and well-balanced food that would help the growth of all children, not just the poor and hungry'.[20]

In 1926 Harold Corry Mann of the Medical Research Council had shown that extra milk had benefited boys in a children's home (in addition to a good diet), increasing their weight and height. Following on this research was John Boyd Orr, of the Rowett Research Institute in Aberdeen, who reported in

Children drinking hot milk at primary school, Lambeth, London, 1929.

The Lancet in 1928 that milk did indeed correlate to an extra 20 per cent increase in weight and height, and improved condition, in his study of 1,400 children aged from five to 14.[21]

But it wasn't the Government that initially ran with the idea of subsidized school milk. Instead, it was the enterprising National Milk Publicity Council (NMPC) – a group of gentlemen, funded by dairy farmers and milk processors, set up to promote and defend the image of milk – that established the first Milk In Schools Scheme (MISS) in 1927, which served a third of a pint to all children at the standard retail price of one penny. By 1934 over one million children in England and Wales were receiving milk through the scheme, totalling nine million gallons per year.[22]

Then there was a potential crisis in the dairy industry due to a surplus of milk production, along with cheap imports of butter and cheese from abroad. It was decided that a government agency, the newly established Milk Marketing Board of

England and Wales (MMB),[23] should take over the administration of MISS to create an official system of school milk provision (intending to expand milk sales).

The re-vamped MISS wasn't an all-out success at first – parents had to pay half a penny for a third of a pint (the rest was subsidized by the government), but by 1938 only 55.6 per cent of state elementary school pupils were participating.[24] Perhaps this was because of the cost to parents, parental indifference or the children not liking the milk.

The milk scheme remained on an uneven keel until the newly created Ministry of Food took over the MISS in 1940 during the Second World War to ensure that rationed milk reached schools. By 1960, and back under the control of the MMB, 82 per cent of children in England and Wales were drinking free milk; 93.4 per cent in primary schools and 66.2 per cent in secondary schools.[25]

Alongside the provision of school milk, the MMB worked hard to promote milk to adults. Backed by nutritional science and government funding, the MMB had to rebrand milk as an enticing and essential food and drink, which they did through publicity campaigns. Increasing milk consumption was essential to the health of the nation – as the chairman of the Scottish Milk Marketing Board declared at the opening of the first milk bar in Glasgow in 1936:

> After the issue of peace and war there was no more important issue before the nation . . . than that of better nutrition, and research had brought [sic] the absolute necessity of greater consumption of liquid milk into the forefront of British public affairs.[26]

But it was a Herculean task to change perceptions about milk that had been held since the nineteenth century.

Milk advertising

One only needs to look at Mrs Beeton's view of milk in the 1860s to see that milk was seen as an ideal food for infants and for invalids (as long as they could digest it):

> This bland and soothing article of diet is excellent for the majority of thin, nervous people; especially for those who have suffered much from emotional disturbances or have relaxed their stomachs by too much tea or coffee, taken too hot.[27]

This staid and unappealing view of milk was still in evidence at the beginning of the twentieth century, with various nutritional studies showing that it was only the young, invalids and the old who drank milk by itself and that adults took their milk in hot drinks and consumed the rest in milk puddings.[28]

Before the MMB took the reins, milk promotion had been in the hands of the NMPC (alongside their Milk in Schools Scheme mentioned previously) since 1922, and their advertising slogan, 'Drink More Milk', was seen from 1924. Not only was milk advertising aimed at children, but also at young women whose looks and health would benefit from a glass of milk a day, and factory workers whose strength and endurance would be increased by drinking milk during their breaks.[29]

Their campaigns were helped during the mid- to late 1930s, when an explosion of milk bars hit London, mainly one Australian franchise known as 'Black and White Milk Bars'. These American-themed imports were gleaming with chrome and formica; serving milk, milkshakes, milk cocktails (with names such as 'Bootlegger's Punch', a 'Goddess Dream' and a 'Blackberry Cocktail'[30]) and ice cream drinks, they aimed at refreshment, but also health and temperance. Although the

Second World War interrupted the rise of the milk bars, they stood milk in good stead as a respectable and enjoyable alternative to alcohol for teenagers and adults. They gave a fresh and hearty image of milk, which 'would encourage adults embarrassed to be seen consuming a drink previously thought to be for children'.[31]

Milk promotion received a huge boost in 1933 when the MMB (remember it was a government agency) took over much of the advertising and direct promotion of milk from the NMPC. It wasn't until after the Second World War that the two groups created their most successful campaigns, including using the slogan 'Drinka Pinta Milka Day' (which appeared from 1958),

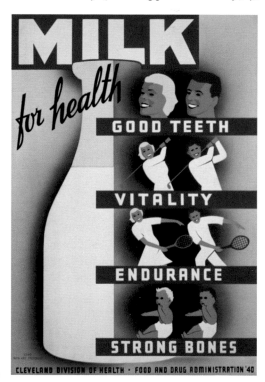

'Milk for Health', 1940. The following pages show a series of 1940s WPA Art Program posters for the Cleveland Division of Health promoting milk for all round well-being.

to encourage regular milk drinking. One campaign that created rather a stir (and a snigger) but did get the message across was the 'Drive Safely on Milk' campaign of 1961. The NMPC had anticipated the coming of the breathalyser by promoting the beneficial effects of drinking a glass of milk immediately before or after a party to prevent a hangover the following day.

Thanks to the power of advertising, milk became seen as a precious commodity which provided all manner of benefits to the consumer: it made you sleep well at night, ensured a pretty (milky) complexion, made you muscular, provided for a healthy old age and made strong toddlers. Who could resist the lure of milk? It would appear from milk consumption

WPA Art Program poster, 'Milk for Summer Thirst', 1940.

statistics that the advertising worked. By the mid-1950s the UK public had more than doubled their intake of milk since 1938–9 – from 3.4 pints per person per week[32] to 8.4 pints[33] – and this increase continued until 1970, peaking in the mid-1960s at 8.7 pints per person per week.[34]

Milk was revitalized, thanks mainly to the government's public health campaign. The trend was the same in the United States where milk advertising campaigns focused on images of healthy babies and children and, from the 1950s, dairy products were one of the 'Basic Four' food groups hailed by public health officials as the main stay of any balanced, healthy diet. Children were urged to drink four glasses of milk a day.[35]

WPA Art Program poster, 'Energy Food - Milk for Warmth', 1941.

'Eat These Every Day', poster produced by New York City's WPA Art Program promoting milk as part of a healthy diet, between 1941–3.

One campaign in the US which gained plenty of newspaper coverage was a famous stunt pulled in 1924 by the Chicago Health Department which saw a locomotive engine fuelled by dried milk pull five carriages carrying 200 orphans about ten miles – the implication was that milk had energy and could therefore create power.[36] The nutritional benefits of this economical food were also the focus of generic advertising in many other Western countries.

5
Modern Milk

The shining halo of milk as a government-backed food for the Western nations has been somewhat tarnished since the 1970s and milk has, again, regained its dubious reputation, but not because it carries a disease risk or is impure. It is now an ultra-clean, mass-produced, all-year-round product – it is everything that it should be. However, many modern issues are culminating in milk getting a raw deal and consumers are left wondering whether milk is good or bad for them. But it is not all bad news for milk as previously non-milk drinking countries (in Asia and to a lesser extent Latin America) are turning milk into a global commodity and worldwide consumption of cow's milk is at an all-time high.[1]

Declining consumption in the West

Milk consumption is still highest in the European Union (Scandinavians are the greatest milk users) and other Europe-derived populations (Australia, Canada, New Zealand and the US), compared with the rest of the world. But consumption has not changed, or has fallen since the mid-1960s. In the UK, according to the National Food Survey, milk consumption has fallen from 5.1 pints per person/week in 1974, to 4.5 pints in 1980, and 3.6 pints in 2000 (these figures include school milk and welfare milk).[2] In fact, milk consumption has fallen to pre-war levels again.

So what has caused this trend? It can't be due to lack of advertising by the dairy industry, nor reduced government-backed health campaigns, both of which are still prominent. But by looking at milk advertising since the 1980s, there are clues to the reasons behind the demise of milk consumption as advertisers have tried continually to transform milk's image and reposition it as a food/drink able to fit in with the health concerns of the day.

The largest drop in milk consumption appears to be in 11–18-year-olds and if this trend continues there are concerns that it could lead to a higher risk of osteoporosis and obesity once children reach adulthood.[3] This trend has been largely attributed to the rise in carbonated soft drinks that vie with milk for the teenage market. In 1945 Americans' intake of milk was four times that of carbonated drinks. By 1988 that ratio had been reversed and carbonated drinks consumption was more than twice that of milk.[4] In the UK, one memorable TV advertising campaign from the late 1980s shows two young boys, just in from playing football, going to the fridge for a drink. One of the boys takes some lemonade, while the other decants a large amount of milk into a glass (from a milk bottle). The boy with the lemonade says, 'Milk! Yuk!' to which the milk drinker answers that Ian Rush (the Liverpool United footballer) drinks it and told him that if he didn't drink lots of milk then he'd only be good enough to play for Accrington Stanley (the club lost its league status in 1962). 'Accrington Stanley – who are they?' answers the lemonade boy. 'Exactly', says the milk boy and the boy with the lemonade makes a grab for the milk rather

Milk promoted as the beautifying alternative to fizzy drinks in the US 'Got Milk?' campaign featuring former children's TV star Amanda Bynes.

Olympic gold medallist Dara Torres promotes milk as the athlete's choice.

than his lemonade. The link between milk and athletic ability was clear to any child watching this commercial.

More recently, the 'milk moustache' advertising under the 'Got Milk?' campaign (in the US) and the 'Got the White Stuff?' campaign (in the UK) has used sporting celebrities, such as footballer David Beckham and the boxer Amir Khan, and fictional characters, such as Superman, to link milk to physical strength and growth. Although the message was for teenagers and young people to choose milk over sugary drinks, milk drinking still declined in the target age group. Plans to increase consumption have included the invention of chocolate-flavoured milk, having individual servings of milk in vending machines in schools (so milk sits next to these carbonated drinks) and promoting the research claim that low-fat milk (or chocolate milk) rehydrates the body after a workout better than special-formula energy drinks.[5]

The other major shift in milk advertising has been to promote the benefits of low-fat milk. Ever since the invention of the cream separator in 1871, it has been possible to separate the cream (fat) from the rest of milk. Milk is available in the US as non-fat, skimmed, 1 per cent cream, 2 per cent cream and whole (4 per cent cream) milk. The UK used only to offer skimmed (0.5 per cent fat), semi-skimmed (1.5–1.8 per cent fat) or whole milk (3.5 per cent fat), but has been allowed to market 1 per cent and 2 per cent milk since 1 January 2008 under EU rules. Sainsbury's supermarket was the first to launch its 'own brand' 1 per cent milk in April 2008.[6]

The cream separator has been a godsend for milk's evolution, because nutrient profiling (the science which rates foods according to their nutritional composition) showed that dairy foods are naturally high in saturated fatty acids. Consumption of these saturated animal fats has been linked to a higher risk of developing coronary heart disease via the onset of atherosclerosis and/or the link with obesity and heart disease. This has led to more consumers avoiding whole milk and plumping instead for low-fat options. As one commentator concluded: 'Milk was a victim of the antifat frenzy, and, from a former position of presumed wholesomeness, milk has been recently presumed guilty and has had to prove its innocence.'[7]

Data from the Scottish Milk Marketing Board showed reduced-fat milk consumption increased dramatically from 0.3 pints per person per week in 1983 to 1.56 pints in 1989[8] and appears to be increasing, with up to 75 per cent of milk consumers now regularly using semi-skimmed and skimmed milk.[9]

Not only has milk advertising moved to promoting low-fat milks, but recent US milk advertising has actually urged consumers to 'Milk Your Diet', which relies on nutritional studies that have shown that 'three glasses of low fat or fat free milk a day can help maintain a healthy weight, plus the protein, along with exercise, helps build muscle for a lean body. So eat right, move more and milk your diet.'[10] Low-fat milk is now an aid to weight loss, as well as a way to prevent heart disease. With celebrities such as singer Sheryl Crow and actress Brooke Shields sporting the 'milk moustache', it seems that milk is moving into the realms of being associated with beauty and thinness, as well as athletic ability and growth/strength.

It is a matter of waiting to see whether consumers can be swayed by the 'milk as an aid to weight loss' message, but it seems that despite the dairy industry's attempts to make milk more 'fun' and 'hip', milk remains a drink/food that people feel they 'should' consume, rather than one they like to take. After all, over 90 per cent of US citizens already know that milk is 'good for them', but consumption isn't increasing.[11]

The milk backlash: health concerns

Aside from the issue of milk's fat content, there has also been a huge body of evidence building up to shoot modern milk down as a totally poisonous substance. The publication of *Milk: The Deadly Poison* by Robert Cohen in 1997 was a landmark in the 'milk backlash'. According to Cohen, milk is responsible for a huge number of ailments and diseases, from breast, colon and pancreatic cancer to asthma and childhood diabetes and Cohen's later book, *Milk A–Z* (2001), cites plenty of medical evidence to support his claims.

Animal rights groups have also been trying to convince consumers to stop buying milk on ethical grounds, but some have moved on to question the safety of milk. A poster for The People for the Ethical Treatment of Animals (PETA), which was later taken down by the billboard advertising companies, featured New York's Mayor Rudy Giuliani (who had just announced he had prostate cancer) with a milk moustache and the question 'Got prostate cancer?' as part of their 'Milk Sucks' campaign in 2000.[12]

Perhaps the greatest blow to milk, particularly in terms of intake by children in the US, has been the turnaround by Dr Benjamin Spock. He concluded in the seventh volume of his *Baby and Child Care* (1998) that children under the age of one shouldn't drink cow's milk, only their mother's milk, and that milk and dairy products shouldn't be included in children's diets at all – they didn't need cow's milk to grow up strong and healthy and that parents were better off leaving the milk for the calves. This was completely contrary to Spock's advice since 1946 that milk products should be part of the diet. And the reasons for his conversion? Milk lacks iron and even impairs absorption of iron in children; it causes colic; it is playing a part in childhood-onset diabetes; many children are intolerant of

got sick kids?

Drinking milk contributes to colic, ear infections, allergies, diabetes, obesity and many other illnesses.

PETA PETA.org.uk

PETA's anti-milk US billboard.

milk; and children on a vegetarian diet (Spock's recommendation for children over the age of two) are getting the nutrients (especially calcium) they need from plant-based diets. However, many nutritionists branded the advice as 'absolutely insane' and one stated: 'take milk away from children – I think that's really dangerous. Milk is needed for calcium and vitamin D.'[13]

So why has milk become the enemy again? The principal reason, many raw milk advocates argue, is the fact that the milk we drink today is unrecognizable from the raw product that actually comes out of the cow. One of the advocates in the US is Ron Schmid and his campaign for a return to raw milk consumption is based on the studies of Weston Price, a gentleman who travelled the world in the 1920s and '30s living amongst so-called 'primitive cultures' documenting their diets. Dairy foods were classed as an essential part of their diet (if the cultures kept livestock), and Price saw none of the health problems associated with milk today. Schmid concludes:

> Commercially available milk is terrible . . . No wonder so many people react so poorly when they consume [it]. But suppose you take some healthy, old-fashioned Jersey

Home-grown raw milk: milking the buffalo, Ludhiana in Punjab, India.

cows, that have not been bred to be milk machines, and keep them out at pasture eating fresh green grass most of the time. Take the proper procedures to insure that the milk from those animals is kept pure and clean. The raw milk from those animals is wonderful food for toddlers, young children, adolescents, and adults . . . I've had hundreds of patients of all ages who thought milk was no good for them thrive on the raw milk from healthy grass fed animals.[14]

Is 'milk' really milk?

So, what is so bad about milk today? When raw milk arrives at the processing unit, already cooled to 4/5°C, it is pooled with other milks in huge silos. The following description is an example of how liquid milk for consumption may be

A worker monitoring pasteurization on a dairy farm in Suffolk, England.

processed. The raw milk is always pasteurized using the HTST process already described. Milk sold in supermarkets is then likely to be 'standardized' into certain blends, such as skimmed or semi-skimmed, which means that consumers are unaware of the natural differences in raw milk produced, for example, by the animal's diet. The first part of standardization is to separate the milk into cream and skimmed milk, using a centrifuge that spins at 2,000 rotations per minute. Then a proportion of the cream is added back into the skimmed milk and blended, depending on the standard for the type of milk being produced. Even whole milk, which has an average fat content of 4 per cent by weight, will have some cream removed if it is 'standardized' to the minimum fat content of 3.5 per cent (in Europe) or 3.25 per cent (in the US). Fat-free and most reduced-fat milks have to be 'fortified' with vitamins to replace the fat-soluble vitamins that disappear along with the cream (vitamin A and D especially). Often milk is then homogenized, which involves breaking down the fat molecules in milk by forcing them through a narrow opening on to a hard surface and reducing them all to the same size. This means that the fat is evenly distributed throughout the milk, stopping a layer of cream from forming on the top. This process is mainly for aesthetic purposes when the milk is packed in transparent poly bottles.

Many critics will say that milk processed in this way cannot possibly taste the same as fresh milk does because it has been tampered with too much. One cheese-maker describes the processing of milk as 'taking it apart and putting it together again as people think it ought to be.'[15] Pasteurization has been accused of producing 'stale, burn-on flavours' in milk and of not only killing harmful bacteria, but also the 40–50 different strains of bacteria that make up the flavour of fresh milk.[16] Additional homogenization has further been accused of reducing the 'creaminess' of milk and resulting in an even blander end product. However, Ultra Heat Treated (UHT) milk leads milk sales in many European countries, especially Belgium, Spain and France, so many 'milk' consumers are enjoying a product which is far removed from its natural state.

But it is not just the taste of modern milk which critics condemn, but also the pasteurization process, which they say reduces the nutritional value of milk. Confusion reigns over this issue, with the industry, government agencies and nutritionists denying that pasteurization has any appreciable effect on milk's nutritional composition.

However, one thing is clear. One only needs to look at the milk section in a relatively small neighbourhood foodstore in New York's Upper East Side to find 30 to 40 different versions of milk: from organic and 'rBST-free'(see below) to vitamin D- and vitamin A-enriched and lactose-reduced milk.[17] The claim that 'milk' is not longer milk does seem to have some substance. And all the processing is far removed from the ancient Indian advice to simply drink raw milk, which hasn't been stored for long, and has preferably been boiled with spices.

Technological milk

The other concern levelled at modern milk is the result of consumer demand. Milk producers have turned to science to find ways to 'improve' the milk yields of dairy cattle, with research focusing on improved animal nutrition, genetic selection of high yielding cattle and improved infection control in the dairy herds.

One issue in the US stands out from the technological crowd: that of a protein called recombinant bovine somatotropin (called either rBGH or rBST), which is a genetically engineered form of a naturally occurring growth hormone in cattle. The protein, produced naturally in the cow's pituitary gland, is injected into cattle and increases milk production by 10–15 per cent in most animals. Not only do critics believe the growth hormone is bad for animal welfare, but, because it is

The huge selection of milks on sale in a supermarket in Taipei, Taiwan, 2008.

genetically engineered, they believe there are question marks over the safety of subsequent milk on human health. Since rBST became commercially available in 1994, under the trade name of POSILAC and manufactured by Monsanto, its use in the US national herd has sparked huge controversy (or at least perceived controversy[18]), culminating in milk that has not been produced using POSILAC being labelled as 'rBST-free' to assist consumers in choosing their preferred milk supply. Many of the main grocery stores now guarantee their own-brand milk as rBST-free, including Kroger and Wal-Mart, and coffee giant Starbucks pledged to be free of rBST in 2007. As a possible result of this consumer backlash, Monsanto announced in August 2008 that they were looking at 'repositioning' (selling) the POSILAC brand name – Elanco have taken on this seemingly poisoned chalice.

The next biotechnological concern with milk is looming on the horizon: that of milk produced from high yielding, cloned cattle entering the food chain. It is unlikely that milk from cloned cattle will be labelled as such, because the Food and Drug Administration (FDA) in the US has concluded that the milk from cloned animals has exactly the same composition as 'normal milk' and so does not need to be labelled. The FDA also concluded in January 2008 that the milk from cloned dairy cattle is 'as safe as . . . [milk] we eat every day.'[19] There has been a similar stance from the European Food Safety Authority (EFSA), although it remains to be seen whether consumers, and the dairy industry, feel the same way. If milk from cloned animals is not labelled, there are industry fears that consumers may decide to reduce their overall milk consumption to be safe. Many companies, such as Kraft Foods, Campbell Soup Company and Gerber/Nestlé, have supported a pledge not to use products sourced from cloned animals, if they can be identified.

Raw milk

Against this backdrop of consumer concerns about how their milk is produced, what it contains and how it is processed, it may be no surprise that sales of raw, or unpasteurized, milk have recently increased. However, consumption still only accounts for less than 1 per cent of all household milk sales, and this could be because it is difficult to source raw milk, since medical and public health officials see it as a dangerous source of bacteria.

In England and Wales, since 1999, it has been illegal to sell raw milk directly to consumers unless the producer holds a licence from DEFRA (the Department for Environment, Food and Rural Affairs) and clearly labels it: 'This milk has not been heat treated and may therefore contain organisms harmful to health.' Sales of untreated milk were banned totally in Scotland in 1983. In the US, raw milk sales are illegal in 18 states and in four others raw milk can only be sold as pet food, and

Raw milk has to come with a health warning.

even then there are proposals (in Georgia) to dye the raw milk a charcoal colour to make it unappetising for humans who may be tempted to break the law.[20] From 1987, the FDA banned the sale of raw milk for human consumption across state lines, because 'raw milk, no matter how carefully produced, may be unsafe'[21] and in 2007, legislation was passed in California which set strict bacterial standards on raw milk sales (producers are currently fighting to overturn the standard).[22] However, there are ways and means to circumvent legislation: Australians wishing to sell raw milk to the public have taken to labelling their milk as 'Bath Milk', but the Government are currently trying to close this loophole.

It is perhaps no surprise that Western sales of milk are declining when modern consumers are constantly barraged with contrary messages to drink, and not to drink milk – is it a 'white poison' or a 'white elixir'? All this sounds horribly familiar. However, it is not all bad news for milk.

Increasing consumption of whole milk in the East

While milk consumption has remained static or fallen in the West during the last 40 years, the opposite is true in Asia, where traditionally non-milk drinking cultures have embraced the white liquid. China's consumption increased a massive 15 times from 1964–2004, while Thailand increased by half that, with India, Japan and the Philippines experiencing a tripling or quadrupling of consumption.[23]

Although milk consumption in Asia is much lower than the West (only two or three per cent of that used in the US[24]), the market is growing rapidly for several reasons. Most emphasis has been placed on the increasing incomes of these

Asian countries, which seems to go hand-in-hand with a demand for milk and other animal-sourced foods. This demand has been created by marketing, which promotes milk as *the* food for growing and athletic children, as well as making milk attractive to Asian societies – mainly working on the desire of increasingly affluent countries to incorporate Western foods into their diets. Or perhaps it is just that milk is more available and cheaper than before and people have started to try dairy products?

In Japan, where the Asian milk boom first started, Japanese children were given milk to drink every morning at school – in fact, it was the school milk programme which was instrumental in stimulating demand for milk in the country – and China has followed suit, with Premier Wen Jiabao announcing in 2007: ' I have a dream to provide every Chinese, especially children, sufficient milk each day.'[25] There is even a World School Milk Day (initiated in 2000) held on the last Wednesday in September in over 30 countries, which shows the extent to which milk is now provided, either at full-cost, subsidized or free, to school children.[26]

As for the 'nutritional colonization' of Asian countries, people are being encouraged by TV advertising campaigns to mix up a suspension of white powdered milk (derived from European milk) and water to pour over cereals – something very much associated with the Western diet and marketed by multinational companies.[27]

Apart from milk on cereals and milk in schools, the greatest increase in milk consumption is seen in milk-based probiotic drinks, such as Yakult (a yoghurt-type drink developed in the 1930s in Japan), ready-made milk tea and milk drinks; Asian consumers drank 13 per cent more milk drinks (especially flavoured milk) in 2007 than in 2006, mainly due to demand in China.[28] The Taiwanese have been guzzling

'Bubble Tea' (also known as boba, pearl tea, milk tea or bubble drink) since the 1980s – its basic and original contents are chilled black tea, milk, honey, ice and tapioca pearls (or balls), all shaken together. But it is not only fresh milk that is used in Asian milky drinks. In Malaysia, Singapore and Brunei they drink a type of tea called *teh tarik* made from tea and condensed milk, which is rather like cappuccino because of its frothy top. It is made by pouring the liquid back and forth between a container held high, into a container held low.

Disparities in supply of, and demand for, milk

When milk consumption is looked at on a global scale, there is an increase in demand of about 3 per cent each year, which is well ahead of milk production.[29] It is left to countries with over-production to make up deficits in other countries; for example, Australia is exporting skimmed milk powder to the Middle East. Even Western countries are facing a shortage of milk because, for example, UK dairy farmers are exiting the industry for many reasons, including high costs, an aging workforce and cattle losses due to tuberculosis,[30] and Asian countries do not yet have the national dairy herd capacity, the access to imports nor the ability to increase forage supply to meet demand. This means that until supply meets demand, global milk prices are likely to rise.

As a solution to the current disparity in demand and supply of milk, several solutions present themselves: production per cow will have to increase, other sources of non-cow milk will have to expand or demand for cow's milk will have to reduce.

Teh tarik or 'pulled tea' being made in Bangkok, Thailand.

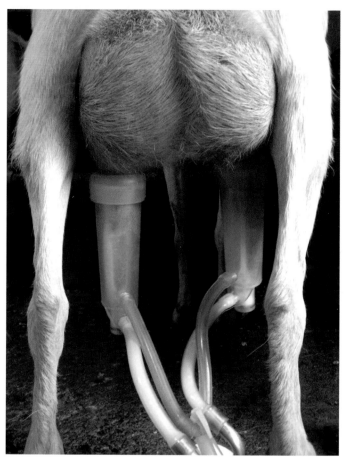

Goat's milk is becoming industrialized and is increasing in popularity.

Dairy research is continually trying to increase milk yields in cattle, but putting 'extreme demands' on dairy cows does have ethical and moral dilemmas attached, of which consumers should be aware.[31] As for non-cow milk, the International Dairy Federation (IDF) reported in 2007 that buffalo milk production had increased by 37 per cent over the previous decade, goat milk had increased by 3.3 per cent and sheep milk by 4.9 per cent over the same period, while production of camel, yak and reindeer milk had remained static.[32] Some increases, such as in sheep and goat's milk, may be due to these milks having a lower lactose content than cow's milk, making it more suitable for people with a perceived intolerance to cow's milk. But, warned the IDF, non-cow's milk 'will remain a niche market simply because of the limited volumes of milk production, which cannot be increased to, or even beyond, the rate of predicted increase of cow's milk'.[33]

So, perhaps, global demand for milk will have to reduce. And this will please environmental campaigners, such as the Food Climate Research Network, based at the University of Surrey, England, who are calling for consumers in developed countries to be rationed to one litre of milk per week (2.1 pints) by 2050 in order to avoid run-away climate change. This amount of milk is the average level of consumption for people in the developing world, and equates to just enough milk to cover a bowl of cereal each day, or about three modest cheese sandwiches a week.[34] The reasoning behind this idea is that cattle (and other livestock) account for most of the emissions of methane from UK food production – in the form of belching and flatulence – and less milk consumption means fewer cattle in the world.

The future of milk?

It is more than likely that milk will continue to enjoy its controversial reputation and remain in the public eye – usually for the wrong reasons. This can be seen in a recent example where human intervention has blackened the pure image of milk. Harking back to the days of contaminated and adulterated

Roadside fresh milk dispenser in Annecy-Le-Vieux, southeastern France, 2009.

milk in the nineteenth century, in September 2008 there was a worldwide scandal involving Chinese milk products that were found to contain melamine (a banned, industrial chemical usually used in paints and plastics). The melamine was added to watered-down milk to make it appear higher in protein and when fed to babies via milk powders, the additive was blamed for causing severely impaired kidney function and painful kidney stones. As at July 2009, at least six Chinese babies have died and over 300,000 babies have been treated in hospital.[35]

There is no doubt that milk – love it or loathe it – will continue to be one of the most widely debated foods in the history of mankind.

Recipes

Milk and Honey Bath
A 'modern version' of Cleopatra's milk bath[1]
—Adapted from Stephanie Rosenbaum's *Honey: From Flower to Table*
(San Francisco, 2002)

90 g powdered milk
4 tbsp honey

Mix the milk and honey into a paste, then dissolve this in a warm bath as you run it.

Salmon and Custard Soup
– taken from the *Bird's Cookery Book*, cited in Alice Thomas Ellis's
Fish, Flesh and Good Red Herring (London, 2004)

1 quart [950 ml] of milk
1 oz [25 g] butter
small tin of salmon
2 pint-packets of Bird's Custard Powder
1½ tsp salt
pepper to taste

Mix the custard powder with three tablespoons of the milk, boil the remainder and pour onto the paste, then stir in the melted butter and season. Remove the skin and bones of the salmon, mash well and mix with the sauce. Reheat and serve at once.

Milk Punch
— from Paul Clarke at www.seriouseats.com

1 oz [30 ml] brandy
1 oz [30 ml] dark rum
1 tsp sugar
2 dashes vanilla extract (optional)
4–6 oz [120–80 ml] whole milk, to taste

Stir well with ice and strain into a large goblet over fresh crushed ice (or, pour everything into a mug and add hot milk). Sprinkle with nutmeg.

Milk Paint Formula (1870) – DO NOT EAT!
by the Real Milk Paint Company [2]

1 quart [950 ml] skim milk (room temperature)
1 oz [25 g] of hydrated lime by weight
1–2½ lb [400 g–1 kg] of chalk (may also be added as a filler)

Stir in enough skim milk to the hydrated lime to make a cream. Add balance of skim milk. Now add sufficient amount of powder pigment to desired colour and consistency – the figment powder must be lime-proof. Stir in well for a few minutes before using and continue to stir throughout use. Extra paint may be kept for several days in the refrigerator, until the milk sours.

Cajeta Mexicana (Mexican Dulce de Leche)
—Adapted from Anne Mendelson, *Milk: The Surprising Story of Milk Through the Ages* (New York, 2008)

1 quart [950 ml] whole cow's milk
1 quart [950 ml] goat's milk
2 cups [400 g] sugar
¼ tsp baking soda

Add the milks to a large, deep (preferably) enamelled cast-iron pan. Remove ½ cup of the milk and reserve. Stir in the sugar with a wooden spoon until dissolved and bring to a low boil. Remove the pan from the heat and stir the baking soda into the reserved ½ cup milk and add it to the hot milk, which will froth up. Return pan to the heat and continue to cook the milk, stirring often, for about 30 minutes. It will start to look like syrup.

Now you must stir constantly, gradually reducing the heat as the syrup darkens and thickens, for another 30 minutes. When a stroke of the mixing spoon exposes the bottom of the pan and the syrup is slow to close in again over the tracks, remove the pan from the heat.

Let it sit until the molten milk-syrup is partly cooled, but still liquid enough to pour into small containers. Let it cool to room temperature before covering. It will keep for weeks at room temperature or in the refrigerator.

Koya Gobhi Mattar (White Curry)
—Adapted from Pat Chapman, *Indian Restaurant Cookbook* (London, 1984)

1 medium onion, finely chopped
sesame or sunflower oil
½ cup cashew nuts, blanched to remove skins and ground
½ cup double cream
2 tbsps milk powder
1 large cauliflower, in florets, parboiled

1 cup peas, fresh or frozen
salt
1 tbsp chopped fresh coriander
½ tsp fennel seeds, coarsely ground
1 tsp sesame seeds
½ tsp coriander, ground

Soften the onions, while making a paste from the nuts, cream, milk powder and spices (adding water if needed to get a thick consistency). Combine the onion, paste and the vegetables and simmer the mixture for up to 10 minutes. Add a little salt, and some water if needed. Garnish with fresh coriander.

Glossary

Types of heat-treated milk

All milk sold via supermarkets, grocers and milkmen must be heat-treated:

Pasteurized milk: contains no harmful bacteria and its nutritional value and taste is not significantly different from raw milk.

Sterilized milk: prolonged heat treatment kills nearly all bacteria in it, which results in changes to the taste and the colour of the milk (it turns slightly brown and has a 'burnt' twang) and reduces its nutritional value. However, unopened bottles or cartons of sterilized milk can keep for several months without refrigeration.

Ultra-High Temperature or Ultra-Heat Treated (UHT) milk: short exposure to very high heat kills off all harmful microorganisms and the milk is packaged into sterile containers. Its flavour is less affected than sterilized milk and, again, keeps without refrigeration. This type of milk is very popular in Europe (but not in Britain): in Belgium, UHT has 96.7 per cent of the market share, in Spain it accounts for 95.7 per cent and in France it makes up 95.5 per cent of all milk sales.

Filtered milk: milk goes through an extra fine filtration system, which removes souring bacteria so the shelf life of the milk is increased way beyond the normal 5 days of pasteurized milk.

The basic types of milk

Whole/full-fat: milk straight from the animal (and pasteurized) with nothing removed, and nothing added. It has an average fat content of 4 per cent.

Whole standardized milk: whole milk which has had some fat removed to meet a minimum fat content of 3.5 per cent (EU) and 3.25 per cent (US).

Whole homogenized milk: whole milk that has been subjected to the homogenization process which breaks up the fat globules in the milk, distributing the fat evenly through the milk and preventing a cream layer forming on the top (most types of milk are now homogenized).

2 per cent milk: has a fat content of 2 per cent.

Semi-skimmed: the most popular milk type in the UK; has a fat content of 1.5–1.8 per cent.

1 per cent milk: has a fat content of 1 per cent.

Skimmed milk: has a fat content of between 0.1–0.3 per cent, therefore nearly all the fat content of whole milk is removed.

Fat-free: milk with all the fat removed; also known as 'skim milk'.

Milk products

Whey: the liquid remaining after milk has been curdled and strained.

Curds: the thick curdled milk remaining after straining.

Buttermilk: the liquid remaining after butter has been churned from the cream, or made from pasteurized skimmed milk to which a culture of lactic acid bacteria is added.

Evaporated milk: a concentrated, sterilized form of milk that has a final concentration twice that of the original milk. The milk is evaporated under pressure and homogenized. The milk is then poured into cans, which are sterilized at high temperatures.

Condensed milk: a sweetened form of evaporated milk, concentrated to three times that of the orginal milk, which is not sterilized. Preservation occurs due to the high concentration of sugar in the milk.

Dried milk powder: the powder produced by evaporating the water from the milk using heated rollers or drying a fine mist of milk.

Acidophilus milk: milk to which a beneficial bacterium*, Lactobacillus acidophilus*, has been added. The bacterium is bile-resistant and helps to relieve the symptoms of lactose maldigestion.

Fortified milk: milk with vitamin D, vitamin A (these fat-soluble vitamins are removed along with the milk fats) and/or calcium added. Milk solids, such as protein and carbohydrates, can also be added to give a 'creamier' taste to low-fat milks.

Reduced lactose milk: milk that is treated with the enzyme *lactase* to reduce its lactose content by about 70 per cent.

Low sodium milk: 95 per cent or more of the sodium that occurs naturally in milk is removed and replaced with potassium.

Flavoured milk: milk to which a flavouring (e.g. cocoa or cocoa powder, strawberry or vanilla extract) and a sweetener has been added.

DHA-enriched milk: milk that comes from cows fed on a diet enriched with DHA from natural sources. DHA is an essential omega-3 fatty acid that develops and maintains the brain, nervous system and retinal health.

Appendix

Composition of Milk by Animal Species

	WATER (%)	PROTEIN (%)	FAT (%)	MILK SUGAR (%)
Camel	85.6	3.7	4.9	5.1
Cow (Holstein)	87.8	3.1	3.5	4.9
Goat	88	3.1	3.5	4.6
Human	87.4	1.1	4.5	6.8
Mare	89	2.7	1.6	6.1
Reindeer	63.3	10.3	22.5	2.5
Sheep	83.7	5.5	5.3	4.6
Water Buffalo	78.5	5.9	10.4	4.3

(Adapted from Robert Bremel, University of Wisconsin:
Milk: Beyond the Dairy, Proceedings of the Oxford
Symposium on Food and Cookery, 1999)

References

1 The First Milk

1 Layinka M. Swinburne, 'Milky Medicine and Magic', in
   *Milk: Beyond the Dairy – Proceedings of the Oxford Symposium on
   Food and Cookery, 1999* (Devon, 2000), p. 337.
2 For more information about the composition and synthesis
   of milk, see the University of Illinois website:
   http://classes.ansci.uiuc.edu/ansc438/Milkcompsynth/mil
   kcompsynthresources.html, as accessed 01/11/08.
3 J. Bostock and H. T. Riley, trans., *The Natural History* by
   Pliny the Elder (London, 1855), Book XXVIII:33 – the
   reduced amount of roughage in lush, new grass reduces the
   fat content of the milk.
4 Samuel Pepys, *The Diary of Samuel Pepys*, vol. VIII [1667], ed.
   Robert Latham and William Matthews (Berkeley, CA, 2000),
   entry for 21 November 1667, p. 543.
5 M. L. Ryder, *Sheep and Man* (London, reprinted 2007), p. 725.
6 The inability to empty the bowels during defecation.
7 Bostock and Riley, trans., Pliny the Elder, *The Natural
   History*, Book XXVIII:33.
8 Valerie Porter, *Yesterday's Farm: Life on the Farm 1830–1960*
   (Newton Abbot, Devon, 2006), p. 224.
9 Laura Barton, 'Go Green at the Coffee Shop – Just Ask for
   a Skinny Decaff Ratte', *Guardian*, Comment and features

section, 21 November 2007, p. 2.

10 Research by the late Andrew Sherratt at the University of Sheffield; cited in R. Mukhopadhyay, 'The Dawn of Dairy', *Analytical Chemistry*, 1 November 2008, p. 7906 (published on the internet at http://pubs.acs.org/doi/pdf/10.1021/ac801789k, as accessed 23/12/08).

11 Professor Andrew Sherrat and Professor Richard Evershed can be heard on Radio 4, Thursday 26 February 2004 talking about their researches into milk on *The Material World*, hosted by Quentin Cooper. Listen again at www.bbc.co.uk/radio4/science/thematerialworld_20040226.shtml, as accessed 06/11/08.

12 See Mukhopadhyay, 'The Dawn of Dairy', p. 7907.

13 Alan Davidson, *Oxford Companion to Food* (Oxford, 1999), p. 503.

14 See www.the-ba.net/the-ba/News/FestivalNews/_FestivalNews2007/_horsemilk.htm, as accessed 22/07/08.

15 E. C. Amoroso and P. A. Jewell, 'The Exploitation of the Milk-Ejection Reflex by Primitive Peoples', in *Man and Cattle: Proceedings of a Symposium on Domestication* (Royal Anthropological Institute, 1963), p. 126.

16 Aubrey de Sélincourt, trans., Herodotus, *The Histories* (London, 2003), Book IV:2, p. 240.

17 F. E. Zeuner, 'The History of the Domestication of Cattle', in *Man and Cattle*, p. 13.

18 Ryder, *Sheep and Man*, p. 725.

19 Ibid., p. 724.

20 Cited in Andrea S. Wiley, 'Transforming Milk in a Global Economy', *American Anthropologist*, CIX/4, p. 670.

21 The ability to digest lactose past adulthood has been traced to a mutant version of the LCT gene, which somehow disabled the off-switch for lactase production. Descendents of these milk-drinkers also carried the mutation.

22 Ryder, *Sheep and Man*, p. 725.

23 Cherry Ripe, 'Animal Husbandry and Other Issues in the Dairy Industry at the End of the Twentieth Century', *Milk: Beyond the Dairy*, p. 298.

24 Najmieh Batmanglij, 'Milk and its By-products in Ancient Persia and Modern Iran', *Milk: Beyond the Dairy*, p. 64.

25 Exodus 23:19, 34:26 and Deuteronomy 14:21.

26 All references to ancient Indian medicine taken from www.mapi.com/ayurveda health_care/newsletters/ayurveda_&_milk.html, as accessed 16/12/08.

27 Figures cited in 'India Bans Milk Products from China' (*India Post.com* website, 28.09.08), www.indiapost.com/article/india/3984/, as accessed 09/12/08.

28 Anne Mendelson, *Milk: The Surprising Story of Milk through the Ages* (New York, 2008), p. 14.

29 2006 figures cited at www.pastoralpeoples.org/docs/06VivekanandanSEVA.pdf, as accessed 12/12/08.

30 Details of yak milk products found on the FAO website: www.fao.org/DOCREP/006/AD347E/ad347e0l.htm, as accessed 17/12/08.

31 William Davis Hooper and Harrison Boyd Ash, trans., Marcus Terentius Varro, *On Agriculture* (London, 1967) Book II, Chapter 11:1.

32 From W. W. Rockhill, trans., *The Journey of William of Rubruck to the Eastern Parts of the World, 1253–5* (London, 1900), http://depts.washington.edu/silkroad/texts/rubruck.html#kumiss, as accessed 12/12/08.

33 Benedict Allen, *Edge of Blue Heaven: A Journey through Mongolia* (London, 1998), p. 74.

34 From Rockhill, trans., *The Journey of William of Rubruck*.

35 For more details see Yagil et al., 'Science and Camel's Milk Production' (1994) at www.vitalcamelmilk.com/pdf/yagil-1994.pdf, pp. 3–4, as accessed 17/12/08.

36 Bostock and Riley, trans., Pliny the Elder, *The Natural History*, Book XI:96.

37 Cited on Bedouin Camp website at www.dakhlabedouins.com/bedouin_healing.html, as accessed 17/12/08.

38 Cited at the 'Sámi Information Centre' website: www.eng.samer.se/GetDoc?meta_id=1203, as accessed 17/12/08.

39 Carol A. Déry, 'Milk and Dairy Products in the Roman

Period', *Milk: Beyond the Dairy*, p. 11.

40 George Rawlinson, ed. and trans., *The History of Herodotus*, vol. III (New York, 1885), 4:2.

41 Julius Caesar, trans. W. A. McDevitte and W. S. Bohn, *Commentaries on the Gallic War* (New York, 1869), 5:14.

42 Déry, 'Milk and Dairy Products in the Roman Period', p. 11.

43 Bostock and Riley, trans., Pliny the Elder, *The Natural History*, Book xx:44.

44 H. G. Bohn, trans., *The Epigrams of Martial* (London, 1865), 13.38.

45 Bostock and Riley, trans., Pliny the Elder, *The Natural History*, Book xxviii:33.

46 Déry, 'Milk and Dairy Products in the Roman Period', p. 121.

47 Ibid., p. 122.

48 Ibid, p. 120.

49 C. Anne Wilson, *Food and Drink in Britain: From the Stone Age to the 19th Century* (Chicago, IL, 1991), p. 149.

50 William Harrison, *A Description of Elizabethan England* (1577), Chapter XII:7.

51 John Burnett, *Liquid Pleasures: A Social History of Drinks in Modern Britain* (London, 1999), p. 29.

52 Keith Thomas, *Man and the Natural World: Changing Attitudes in England 1500–1800* (London, 1984), p. 94.

53 Cited in Patricia Monaghan, *The Red-Haired Girl from the Bog: The Landscape of Celtic Myth and Spirit* (California, 2004), p. 176.

54 Ibid., p. 176.

55 Patricia Aguirre, 'The Culture of Milk in Argentina', *Anthropology of Food*, 2 September 2003, http://aof. revues.org/document322.html, as accessed 03/04/09.

56 See discussion in G. A. Bowling, 'The Introduction of Cattle into Colonial North America', p. 140, at http:// jds.fass.org/cgi/reprint/25/2/129.pdf, p. 140, as accessed 18/12/08.

57 Ibid., p. 140.

2 The 'White Elixir'

1 M. J. Rosenau, *The Milk Question* (Cambridge, 1912), p. 6.
2 Cassandra Eason, *Fabulous Creatures, Mythical Monsters and Animal Power Symbols* (London, 2008), pp. 89–91.
3 J. Bostock and H. T. Riley, trans., Pliny the Elder, *The Natural History* (London, 1855), Book XIV:88.
4 DeTraci Regula, *The Mysteries of Isis: Her Worship and Magick* (Saint Paul, MN, 1995), pp. 162–3.
5 Hilda M. Ransome, *The Sacred Bee in Ancient Times and Folklore* (New York, 2004), p. 276.
6 Chitrita Banerji, 'How the Bengalis Discovered *Chhana*' in *Milk: Beyond the Dairy – Proceedings of the Oxford Symposium on Food and Cookery* (Devon, 2000), pp. 49–50.
7 Ibid., p. 50.
8 Hilda Ellis Davidson, *Roles of the Northern Goddess* (London, 1998), pp. 36–7.
9 Layinka M. Swinburne, 'Milky Medicine and Magic', in *Milk: Beyond the Dairy*, p. 338.
10 Cited in Thomas Keightley, *The Fairy Mythology*, vol. I (London, 1833), p. 110.
11 An Oxonian, *Thaumaturgia, or Elucidations of the Marvellous* (Oxford, 1835), p. 24.
12 Cited in E. C. Amoroso and P. A. Jewell, 'The Exploitation of the Milk-Ejection Reflex by Primitive Peoples', in *Man and Cattle: Proceedings of a Symposium on Domestication* (Royal Anthropological Institute, 1963), p. 135.
13 Bostock and Riley, trans., Pliny the Elder, *The Natural History*, Book XXVIII:33.
14 Ibid.
15 Cited in Layinka M. Swinburne, 'Milky Medicine and Magic', p. 341.
16 Ibid., p. 337.
17 Pope cited in Sir Egerton Bydges *Collins's Peerage of England*, vol. IV (London, 1812), p. 156.
18 W. J. Gordon, *The Horse World of London* (London, 1893), pp. 174–5.

19 Margaret Forster, *Elizabeth Barrett Browning* (London, 1988), p. 365.

20 From the *Bulletin de l' Académie de Médecine*, 1882, cited at www.asinus.fr/histoire/info.html, as accessed 17/07/08.

21 Anon., 'The Physician A-Foot', *The Times*, 13 September 1850, p. 7.

22 Anon., 'Massolettes and Sour Milk', *The Times*, 10 March 1910, p. 9.

23 Bernarr MacFadden, *The Miracle of Milk: How to Use the Milk Diet Scientifically at Home* (1935) – copy of text at www.milk-diet.com/classics/macfadden/macfaddenmain.html, as accessed 14/12/08.

24 Bostock and Riley, trans., Pliny the Elder, *The Natural History*, Book XI:96 and Book XXVIII:50.

25 Steven S. Braddon, 'Consumer Testing Methods', in *Skin Moisturization*, ed. James J. Leyden and Antony V. Rawlings (New York, 2002), p. 435.

26 Ibid., p. 436.

27 George P. Marsh, *The Camel: Organization, Habits and Uses* (New York, 1856), p. 75.

3 White Poison

1 Colin Spencer, *British Food: An Extraordinary Thousand Years of History* (London, 2002), p. 162.

2 Samuel Pepys, *The Diary of Samuel Pepys: 1668–1669*, ed. Robert Latham and William Matthews (Berkeley, CA, 2000), entry for 20 May 1668, p. 207.

3 John Burnett, *Liquid Pleasures: A Social History of Drinks in Modern Britain* (London, 1999), p. 30.

4 William Cobbett, *Cottage Economy* (London, 1828), 'Keeping Cows: 113'.

5 Burnett, *Liquid Pleasures*, p. 32.

6 Peter Quennell, ed., *Mayhew's London* (London, 1984), p. 131.

7 Cited in P. J. Atkins, 'White Poison? The Social Consequences of Milk Consumption, 1850-1930', *Social*

History of Medicine, V (1992), p. 226.

8 M. J. Rosenau, *The Milk Question* (Cambridge, 1912), p. 6.

9 Cited in Thomas Beames, *The Rookeries of London* (London, 1852), pp. 214–15.

10 P. J. Atkins, 'London's Intra-Urban Milk Supply circa 1790–1914', *Change in the Town* (Transactions of the Institute of British Geographers, New Series), 11/3 (1977), p. 395.

11 Robert Milham Hartley, *An Historical, Scientific, and Practical Essay on Milk as an Article of Human Sustenance: Consideration of the Effects Consequent Upon the Unnatural Methods of Producing It for the Supply of Large Cities* (New York, 1977), p. 134.

12 Andrew F. Smith, 'The Origins of the New York Dairy Industry', in *Milk: Beyond the Dairy – Proceedings of the Oxford Symposium on Food and Cookery* (Devon, 2000), p. 325.

13 Abraham Jacobi (president of the American Medical Association), cited at www.realmilk.com/untoldstory_1.html, as accessed 24/11/08.

14 William Cobbett, *Cottage Economy*, 'Keeping Cows: 127'.

15 Although Hartley did publish a series of essays in 1836–7.

16 Robert Milham Hartley, *Essay on Milk*, p. 109.

17 Ibid., p. 110.

18 Ibid., p. 125.

19 P. J. Atkins, 'Sophistication Detected: Or the Adulteration of the Milk Supply 1850–1914', *Social History*, XVI (1991), p. 320.

20 Cited in Atkins, 'London's Intra-urban Milk Supply', p. 388.

21 Cited in Burnett, *Liquid Pleasures*, p. 39.

22 Atkins, 'Sophistication Detected', p. 320.

23 Ref: Tobias Smollett – see footnote 31.

24 John Timbs, *Curiosities of London: Exhibiting the Most Rare and Remarkable Objects of Interest in the Metropolis* (London, 1855), p. 49.

25 Jim Phillips and Michael French, 'State Regulation and the Hazards of Milk, 1900–1939', *Social History of Medicine*, XII/3, p. 373.

26 Cited in Atkins, 'White Poison?', pp. 211–12.

27 Atkins, 'London's Intra-Urban Milk Supply', p. 395.

28 Cited in Atkins, 'White Poison?', p. 212.

29 Atkins, 'Sophistication Detected', p. 338.

30 Upton Sinclair, *The Jungle* (New York, 1985), p. 93.

31 Tobias Smollett, *The Expedition of Humphrey Clinker* (New York, 1836), p. 159.

32 Derek Hudson, *Munby: Man of Two Worlds* (London, 1972), p. 250.

33 Atkins, 'London's Intra-Urban Milk Supply', p. 395.

34 Anon., 'Bad Milk', *New York Times*, 30 April 1874.

35 '"Best for Babies" or "Preventable Infanticide"? The Controversy over Artificial Feeding of Infants in America, 1880–1920', *The Journal of American History*, LXX/1 (June 1983), p. 84.

36 See chapter entitled 'Why Not Mother?' in E. Melanie DuPuis, *Nature's Perfect Food: How Milk Became America's Drink* (New York, 2002) pp. 46–66.

37 '"Best for Babies" or "Preventable Infanticide"?', p. 77.

38 Mary F. Henderson, *Practical Cooking and Dinner Giving* (New York, 1887), p. 333.

39 'Milk and its Preservation', *Scientific American*, n.s., 2 July 1860, III, pp. 2–3.

40 See the history of Borden, Inc at www.fundinguniverse. com/company-histories/Borden-Inc-Company-History.html, as accessed 17/11/08.

41 The Anglo-Swiss Company was established in Switzerland in 1866. This company later merged, and was ultimately incorporated into Nestlé.

42 '"Best for Babies" or "Preventable Infanticide"?', p. 78.

43 Burnett, *Liquid Pleasures*, p. 37.

44 See 'Condensed Milk for School Use', at www.milk.com/ wall-o-shame/nutrition/Condensed_Milk.html, as accessed 22/12/08.

45 Alan Jenkins, *Drinka Pinta: The Story of Milk and the Industry that Serves it* (London, 1970), p. 58.

46 Cited in Penny Van Esterik, 'The Politics of Breastfeeding: An Advocacy Perspective', in *Food and Culture: A Reader*, ed. Carole Counihan and Penny Van Esterik (London, 1997),

p. 371. Many breast-feeding advocates cite this speech as the beginning of the movement leading up to the boycott of Nestlé's infant formulas in 1977, after their aggressive sales tactics to Third World countries.

4 Solving the Milk Question

1 Frank Trentmann, 'Bread, Milk and Democracy: Consumption and Citizenship in Twentieth-Century Britain', in *The Politics of Consumption: Material Culture and Citizenship in Europe and America*, ed. Martin J. Daunton and Matthew Hilton (Oxford, 2001), pp. 139–40.

2 M. J. Rosenau, *The Milk Question* (Cambridge, 1912), p. 3.

3 Ibid., p. 297.

4 Cited in P. J. Atkins, 'White Poison? The Social Consequences of Milk Consumption, 1850–1930', *Social History of Medicine*, v (1992), p. 217.

5 The British doctor David Bruce identified *Brucella melitensis* in 1886, which was the bacteria responsible for widespread outbreaks of Malta Fever seen in British soldiers garrisoned on Malta – they were drinking large quantities of goat's milk, which was transmitting the bacteria.

6 Rosenau, *The Milk Question*, pp. 6–7.

7 Ibid., p. 97.

8 '"Best for Babies" or "Preventable Infanticide"? The Controversy over Artificial Feeding of Infants in America, 1880–1920', *The Journal of American History*, lxx/1 (June 1983), p. 86.

9 Although, confusingly, this pasteurized milk was known as 'sterilized' milk, as reported in the *New York Times*, 16 May 1894.

10 Cited on the 'Real Milk' website at www.realmilk.com/untoldstory_1.html, as accessed 25/11/08.

11 For further discussion, see Francis McKee, 'The Popularisation of Milk as a Beverage During the 1930s', in *Nutrition in Britain: Science, Scientists and Politics in the Twentieth*

Century, ed. David F. Smith (Oxford, 1997), p. 125.

12 Cited in 'Milk Must Be Pure Under New Order', *New York Times*, 19 December 1911. See http://query.nytimes.com/mem/archive-free/pdf?res=9900E6D81E31E233A2575AC1A9 649D946096D6CF.

13 For further detail see Trentmann, 'Bread, Milk and Democracy', p. 141.

14 Cited in Atkins, 'White Poison?', p. 226.

15 Cited in Trentmann, 'Bread, Milk and Democracy', p. 142.

16 Cited in Jim Phillips and Michael French, 'State Regulation and the Hazards of Milk, 1900–1939', *Social History of Medicine*, XII/3, p. 376.

17 Ibid., pp. 371–2.

18 Although the National Milk Publicity Council (who ran the early milk schemes) appeared to take great care in providing 'Pasteurized' or raw 'Grade A (TT)' milk to the children, there is no information available on the actual grades of milk used.

19 Atkins, 'White Poison?', p. 226 (fn 91).

20 Peter Atkins, 'The Milk in Schools Scheme, 1934–45: 'Nationalization' and Resistance', *History of Education*, XXXIV/1 (January 2005), p. 2.

21 McKee, 'The Popularisation of Milk as a Beverage During the 1930s', p. 126.

22 Atkins, 'The Milk in Schools Scheme', p. 2.

23 The Milk Marketing Board was established in the Agricultural Marketing Acts of 1931 and 1933 to regulate the marketing of milk. The Board purchased all milk produced and sold it for liquid consumption or manufacture. The income was pooled and proportionally distributed back to producers. It was abolished in 1994.

24 Atkins, 'The Milk in Schools Scheme', p. 5.

25 John Burnett, *Liquid Pleasures: A Social History of Drinks in Modern Britain* (London, 1999), p. 46. This scheme remained in place until 1968 when free milk was withdrawn from secondary schools by a Labour government (justified because of the lower take-up by older pupils). Then in 1971 it was

withdrawn by a Conservative government from elementary school children over seven years old (unless they had a medical certificate). The politician responsible for the cut was Margaret Thatcher (then the Conservative Secretary of State for Education) and the unpopular move gained her the playground taunt of 'Thatcher, Thatcher, Milk Snatcher.'

26 Cited in McKee, 'The Popularisation of Milk as a Beverage During the 1930s', p. 138.

27 Isabella Beeton, *Mrs Beeton's Book of Household Management* (London, 1861), chap. 33, para. 1627.

28 Colin Spencer, *British Food: An Extraordinary Thousand Years of History* (London, 2002), p. 297

29 Alan Jenkins, *Drinka Pinta: The Story of Milk and the Industry that Serves it* (London, 1970), p. 103.

30 'Milk Bars', *The Times*, 4 September 1936, p. 13.

31 McKee, 'The Popularisation of Milk as a Beverage During the 1930s', p. 136.

32 From the *Agricultural Statistics* and *The Statistical Abstract of the United Kingdom* – based on food supply estimates. See D. J. Oddy, 'Food, Drink and Nutrition', in *The Cambridge Social History of Britain, 1750–1950*, ed. F.M.L. Thompson (Cambridge, 1990), p. 268.

33 Based on data from the UK's *National Food Survey, 1942–1996* at https://statistics.defra.gov.uk/esg/publications/nfs/datasets/allfood.xls, as accessed 01/12/08.

34 Ibid.

35 Daniel Ralston Block, 'Hawking Milk: The Public Health Profession, Pure Milk, and the Rise of Advertising in Early Twentieth-century America', in *Milk: Beyond the Dairy – Proceedings of the Oxford Symposium on Food and Cookery* (Devon, 2000), p. 86.

36 Ibid., pp. 90–91.

5 Modern Milk

1 Andrea S. Wiley, 'Transforming Milk in a Global Economy', *American Anthropologist*, CIX/4, p. 666.

2 Data converted from DEFRA statistics at www.statistics.gov. uk/CCI/SearchRes.asp?term=food+consumption, as accessed 01/12/08.

3 L. D. McBean, G. D. Miller and R. P. Heaney, 'Effect of Cow's Milk on Human Health', in *Beverages in Nutrition and Health*, ed. T. Wilson and N. J. Temple (Totowa, NJ, 2004), p. 217.

4 Ibid., p. 214.

5 'Making Good Beverage Choices: Reach for a Glass of Milk After your Next Workout', at www.whymilk.com/ health_choices_workout.php, as accessed 02/12/08.

6 Valerie Elliot, 'Milk Producers Urged to Skim Off More Fat as EU Relaxes Rules', *The Times*, 1 January 2008.

7 McBean, Miller and Heaney, 'Effect of Cow's Milk on Human Health', p. 208.

8 Data taken from Verner Wheelock, ed., *Implementing Dietary Guidelines for Healthy Eating* (London, 1997), p. 229.

9 Elliot, 'Milk Producers Urged to Skim Off More Fat'.

10 See the 'Milk Your Diet' website at www.whymilk.com, as accessed 02/12/08.

11 Wiley, 'Transforming Milk in a Global Economy', p. 675.

12 PETA's 'Milk Sucks' campaign: www.milksucks.com/ index2.asp, as accessed 24/11/08.

13 Dr T. Berry Brazelton cited in Jane E. Brody, 'Final Advice from Dr Spock: Eat Only All your Vegetables', *New York Times*, 20 June 1998.

14 Ron Schmid, 'Nutrition and Weston A. Price' (2003) at www.drrons.com/weston-price-traditional-nutrition.htm, as accessed 03/12/08.

15 Sarah Freeman and Silvija Davidson, 'The Origins of Taste in Milk, Cream, Butter and Cheese', in *Milk: Beyond the Dairy – Proceedings of the Oxford Symposium on Food and Cookery* (Devon, 2000), p. 163.

16 Ibid., p. 163.

17 Cherry Ripe, 'Animal Husbandry and Other Issues in the Dairy Industry at the End of the Twentieth Century', in *Milk: Beyond the Dairy*, p. 297.

18 Terry Etherton, *Transcript: Consumer Awareness of Biotechnology – Separating Fact from Fiction* on the PennState website at http://blogs.das.psu.edu/tetherton/2006/11/06/consumer-awareness-of-biotechnology-separating-fact-from-fiction/, as accessed 05/12/08.

19 On the web at www.fda.gov/cvm/cloning.htm, as accessed 30/05/08.

20 David E. Gumpert, 'Got Raw Milk?', *Boston Globe Sunday Magazine*, 23 March 2008.

21 From the US Food and Drug Administration. Questions and Answers: Raw Milk webpage at www.cfsan.fda.gov/~dms/rawmilqa.html, as accessed 03/12/08.

22 Gumpert, 'Got Raw Milk?'.

23 Wiley, 'Transforming Milk in a Global Economy', p. 668.

24 Ibid., p. 668.

25 See http://news.bbc.co.uk/1/hi/magazine/6934709.stm, as accessed 17/07/2008.

26 Michael Griffin, 'Issues in the Development of School Milk', paper presented at the School Milk Workshop, FAO Intergovernmental Group on Meat and Dairy Products (June 2004). See www.fao.org/es/esc/common/ecg/169/en/School_Milk_FAO_background.pdf, as accessed 02/12/08.

27 Ripe, 'Animal Husbandry and Other Issues', p. 298.

28 See 'Global Growth Potential Lies in Milk and Water Drinks – Report', 15 September 2008 on Dairyreporter.com: www.dairyreporter.com/Industry-markets/Global-growth-potential-lies-in-milk-and-water-drinks-report, as accessed 15/10/08.

29 Figures from Rabobank Group in 2007, cited in Gavin Evans and Danielle Rossingh, 'Got Milk Money? Prices Up as World Wants More Dairy', *Seattle Times*, 25 May 2007.

30 Caroline Stocks and Jeremy Hunt, 'Tough Going as Milk

Production Sinks to a New Low', *Farmers Weekly*, 17 October 2008, p. 24.

31 Hannah Velten, *Cow* (London, 2007), pp. 158–60.

32 Figures cited in Neil Merrett, 'Innovation Required to Milk Sheep and Camel Dairy Potential', on the Food&Drink Europe.com website: www.foodanddrinkeurope.com/ Consumer-Trends/Innovation-required-to-milk-sheep-and-camel-dairy-potential, as accessed 06/12/08.

33 Ibid.

34 David Derbyshire, 'Meat must be Rationed to Four Portions a Week to Beat Climate Change, Says Government-funded Report', *Daily Mail*, 1 October 2008.

35 Figures cited from www.chinadaily.com.cn/bizchina/ 2009-07/13/Content_8422645.htm, as accessed 12/11/09.

Recipes

1 Taken from www.seriouseats.com/recipes/2007/12/ cocktails-milk-punch-recipe.html, as accessed 22/07/08.

2 Taken from The Real Milk Paint Company at www. realmilkpaint.com/recipe.html, as accessed 21/12/08.

Select Bibliography

Burnett, John, *Liquid Pleasures: A Social History of Drinks in Modern Britain* (London, 1999)

DuPuis, E. Melanie, *Nature's Perfect Food: How Milk Became America's Drink* (New York, 2002)

Hartley, Robert Milham, *An Historical, Scientific, and Practical Essay on Milk* (New York, 1977)

Jenkins, Alan, *Drinka Pinta: The Story of Milk and the Industry that Serves it* (London, 1970)

Mendelson, Anne, *Milk: The Surprising Story of Milk through the Ages* (New York, 2008)

Milk: Beyond the Dairy – Proceedings of the Oxford Symposium on Food and Cookery 1999 (Devon, 2000)

Rosenau, M. J., *The Milk Question* (Cambridge, 1912)

Ryder, M. L., *Sheep and Man* (London, 2007)

Spencer, Colin, *British Food: An Extraordinary Thousand Years of History* (London, 2002)

Websites and Associations

Pro-milk

us Why Milk? promotional website
www.whymilk.com

California Milk Processor Board promotional website
www.gotmilk.com

us Milk Processor Education Program
www.bodybymilk.com

uk Dairy Council website
www.milk.co.uk

uk Milk Development Council's website
www.mdc.org.uk

The School Milk Project
www.schoolmilk.co.uk

Anti-milk

Notmilk! US anti-dairy website
www.notmilk.com

People For Ethical Treatment of Animals' anti-milk website
www.milksucks.com

Pro-raw milk

US 'Campaign for Real Milk'
www.realmilk.com

Australia's 'Real Milk' campaign
http://realmilkaustralia.com

Miscellaneous milk

News website covering dairy processing and markets
www.dairyreporter.com

Everything you wanted to know about evaporated milk and
condensed milk
www.verybestbaking.com/products/carnation/
thecookingmilk.aspx

A homage to the humble milk bottle
www.milkbottleoftheweek.com

Guide to making frothy milk
http://coffeegeek.com/guides/frothingguide

Acknowledgements

Thanks to Harry Gilonis for his usual patience, and to all those who contributed their images free of charge.

This book is for my son Cameron, who kept me company throughout the researching and writing of this book – any inaccuracies are due to 'pregnancy brain'.

Photo Acknowledgements

The author and publishers wish to express their thanks to the below sources of illustrative material and/or permission to reproduce it. Locations, etc., of some artworks omitted from the captions for reasons of space are also given below.

Photo © Kangan Arora 2009: p. 108; courtesy of the author: pp. 8 (top), 19, 65, 72; Bodleian Library, Oxford (MS. Bodl. 764): p. 13; British Museum, London (photo © The Trustees of the British Museum): pp. 14–15; photo Cesar Cabrera: p. 36; Camden Local Studies and Archives Centre: p. 49; photo Marion Curtis/Rex Features: p. 103; Dulwich Picture Gallery, London: p. 43; *Farmers Weekly*: p. 11; J. Paul Getty Museum, Los Angeles: p. 56; photo Mike Grenville (www.changingworlds.info): p. 115; photos Clare Hill (www.clarehill.net): pp. 21, 27; photo Jacob P. Jacob: p. 39; photo Helen Jones: p. 32; photo Mark Kerrison: p. 20; photo Pei-Pei Ketron (www.penelopesloom.com): pp. 112–13; Library of Congress, Washington, DC: pp. 61, 62, 86, 88 (Prints and Photographs Division), 81, 95, 96, 97, 98 (Prints and Photographs Division, Work Projects Administration Poster Collection); photo Vrindavan Lila Dasi: p. 40 (top); photo Arthur Macartney: p. 45; photo L. J. and Dave Moore: p. 120; Musée de l'Assistance Publique, Hôpitaux de Paris: p. 87; photo Lawrence Oh: p. 119; photo Pacific Press Service/Rex Features: p. 17; photo David Pearson/Rex Features: p. 8 (bottom); PETA: p. 107; courtesy Pitt Rivers Museum, University of Oxford: p. 24; private collection: p. 78; photo Rex Features:

p. 109; photos Roger-Viollet/Rex Features: pp. 53, 87; from M. J. Rosenau, *The Milk Question* (Boston, MA, 1912): p. 82; from George Augustus Sala, *Twice around the Clock: or, The Hours of the Day and Night in London* (London, 1859): p. 58; photo Sipa Press/Rex Features: p. 122; State Russian Museum, Leningrad: p. 37; photo Topfoto: p. 92; Trinity College, Cambridge (MS R. 17. 1): p. 31; photo wax115/morgueFile: p. 6; photo Christopher Charles White (www.christopherwhitephotography.com): p. 40 (bottom); photo Jeff Wichmann (www.americanbottle.com): p. 84.

Index

italic numbers refer to illustrations; **bold** to recipes